W9-AMQ-391

At Issue

| Domestic Terrorism

Other Books in the At Issue Series:

Published in 2017 by Greenhaven Publishing, LLC
353 3rd Avenue, Suite 255, New York, NY 10010

Articles in Greenhaven Publishing anthologies are often edited for length to meet page
requirements. In addition, original titles of these works are changed to clearly present
the main thesis and to explicitly indicate the author's opinion. Every effort is made to
ensure that Greenhaven Publishing accurately reflects the original intent of the authors.
Every effort has been made to trace the owners of the copyrighted material.

Cover image: [TK]

Library of Congress Cataloging-in-Publication Data

t/k

Manufactured in _____

Website: http://greenhavenpublishing.com

At Issue

| Domestic Terrorism

Elizabeth Schmermund

GREENHAVEN
PUBLISHING

Contents

Introduction

A s peace activist and former hostage of a terrorist group in Beirut, Lebanon, Terry Waite states, "World War Three has already begun." This may seem to be fear mongering at worst, or exaggeration at best, but many in the intelligence community would concur. In recent years, both international and domestic terrorism has increased exponentially. The ubiquitous wars across the Middle East, once so distant to the Western world, have now been delivered to us in the form of terrorist attacks.

In the United States, fears of domestic terrorism are linked with fears of Islamic extremism. And with good reason. The Islamic State, otherwise known as the Islamic State of Iraq and Syria (ISIS), has been busily recruiting people around the globe to carry out "lone wolf" attacks. Many of these new recruits are American citizens or residents, who have spent many years on American soil and have intimately known—and adopted—American culture. Is this incompatible? Not necessarily, according to experts. Islamist groups like ISIS are not as stringent about religious practice as about political practice, and many recruits lack a sense of belonging or have an anger that can only be satisfied in ISIS's endgame. Just as worrisome for the US intelligence community is ISIS's strength in social media marketing and its ability to reach out to many savvy internet users with their message. This gives ISIS unprecedented access to scores of disaffected youths across the Western world who may have a bone to pick with their governments.

But others in the intelligence community and the media don't consider domestic terrorists to be those who are influenced by "outside" ideologies. According to these commentators, domestic terrorism has followed a separate history in the United States. Anarchist terrorism was often labeled as the biggest threat facing the United States at the beginning of the twentieth century, while the mid-twentieth century saw an uptick in another kind of violence: the rise of right-wing extremist groups. These terrorist organizations included the racist Ku Klux Klan, which has a much longer history than other terrorist groups in the United States and deliberately used terrorist tactics in response to the civil rights movement in the 1950s and 1960s. The 1960s and 1970s brought about another shift, with left-wing animal and environmental rights organizations, like the Animal Liberation Front and the Earth Liberation Front, using violent tactics to draw attention to their causes.

But, once again, dominant domestic terrorist groups in the United States have changed in recent years. In his article "Sovereign Citizens Engage in a Wide Range of Terrorist Activity and Must Be Stopped," included in this book, Charles Loeser describes the genealogy of anti-government terrorist organizations, beginning with the Posse Comitatus, a tax protester movement in the 1960s and 1970s, and the militia movement of the 1990s. The militia movement, in particular, instilled terror in the hearts of many Americans during this time. It began largely in response to two deadly sieges: the Waco siege in 1993, in which a law-enforcement investigation of the Branch Davidians religious group led to a fifty-one day siege and culminated in the deaths of seventy-six people; and Ruby Ridge, which pitted law-enforcement officials against anti-government activist Randy Weaver and his family, resulting in three deaths. In fact, Timothy McVeigh and Terry Nichols planned the 1995 bombing of the Alfred P. Murrah Federal Building in Oklahoma City in response to their anger at the federal government for "mishandling" these two sieges. Known as the Oklahoma City Bombing, this domestic terrorist attack killed 168 people and injured over 680 others. This was the deadliest terrorist attack on American soil at the time and remains the deadliest domestic terrorist attack to this day.

Then came September 11, 2001. Following these horrific attacks, the US intelligence community understandably shifted its focus to international terrorism. But, in response to these attacks, the intelligence community also adapted to new "invisible" threats in ways that would have great implications not only for both domestic and international terrorists but also for the American public at large. The US Patriot Act, passed in the immediate aftermath of the September 11 attacks, expanded the definition of domestic terrorism and entrusted the federal government with unprecedented powers to spy on American citizens and obtain private information without warrants. Many organizations, including the American Civil Liberties Union (ACLU), have been highly critical of the US Patriot Act, while the federal government holds that it is the only thing that has allowed Americans relative security in this unstable time. Critics of the Patriot Act have only become more vocal in recent years since former Central Intelligence Agency (CIA) computer specialist Edward Snowden released thousands of classified documents revealing the extent of US government spying on both Americans and non-Americans. This has created a large global debate about the balance of privacy and security. Would you be willing to give up your privacy if there was a chance it would prevent future domestic terrorist attacks?

The US government claims that in the years since 2001, many domestic attacks have been thwarted through the intelligence gathered under the provisions of the Patriot Act. However, there have also been many suspected "terrorists" who have gone to jail due to the stipulations of the act and the new classification of domestic terrorism. In particular, the ACLU has highlighted how peaceful political activists, including both typically right-wing anti-abortion protesters and left-wing environmental activists, could be prosecuted with a crime under the Patriot Act's stipulations. Others, like journalist Jenna McLaughlin, show how the charge of "domestic terrorism" is never used because it is such a broadly defined term that it has actually nullified itself. This could be seen as another critique against this often-criticized act.

Indeed, the term "domestic terrorism" itself is controversial, and conversations involving who should be classified as domestic terrorists and why can often devolve into heated battles, especially during this time of heightened fear. Many on the left of the political spectrum have argued that the term seems to be reserved for nonwhite immigrants and is facilitated by easy access to firearms, while the right worries about the classification of domestic terrorism in regard to the First Amendment. Make no mistake about it: as the French philosopher Michel Foucault noted, the words we use are powerful political tools, and the classification and use of terms such as "domestic terrorism" have wide-ranging consequences. It seems that there must be a trade-off between security and privacy, perhaps even testing the limits of such cherished American liberties as free speech and free expression, but what will those trade-offs be? How can we increase domestic security while also making sure the United States does not become a "security state," in which the basic human rights of certain citizens (for example, Muslim Americans or environmental activists) are denied?

This book offers a range of viewpoints on the topic of domestic terrorism and will hopefully incite you to think more deeply about this important contemporary issue. While some of the commentators included in this text argue that the threat of terrorism in the United States is widely overblown, others express their deep concerns about the viability of these threats. Whatever the case—whether the threat of domestic terrorism is largely invented or it is the most dangerous threat to our lives today—this issue will define future generations. Once, terrorism was far from the minds of everyday American citizens. Unfortunately, this is no longer the case. Terrorism is at the forefront of our attention and our fears and, in many cases, has interfered with how normal people live their lives. Some authors offer solutions in this text, including greater US government outreach among minority communities, although few would state that the US government has reached a consensus on the best path forward.

We hope for a time when terrorism is no longer such a "hot" topic—and perhaps even for a time when a book such as this is no longer needed.

1

The US Freedom Act Continues to Restrict Americans' Freedoms

Jon Queally

Jon Queally is a managing editor and staff writer for Common Dreams, *where he covers many topics, including foreign policy, US politics, and human and animal rights.*

Passed in the wake of the September 11 terrorist attacks, the US Patriot Act redefined how the US government perceived and responded to acts of terrorism, notably expanding the definition of "domestic terrorism." In the years since the Patriot Act was instated, many Americans have critiqued the act for its controversial surveillance practices. Largely in response to these critiques, the USA Freedom Act was enacted on June 2, 2015, following the Patriot Act's expiration. Here, Jon Queally describes some of the changes in "domestic spying" provided in this act, while giving voice to those who continue to critique the surveillance of American citizens in the name of security against terrorism. In particular, the vague "material support provision" continues to trouble civil rights activists.

A bipartisan bill, designed to rein in the bulk collection of the private communications of American citizens, was introduced Tuesday by members of the House and Senate Judiciary Committees, ahead of an upcoming expiration date for key Patriot Act provisions that have given legal authority to some of the most controversial domestic surveillance practices revealed over the last two years.

With a June 1 expiration for Sections 206 and 215 of the USA Patriot Act, initially rammed through Congress in the wake of the attacks of September 11, 2001, the revisions contained in the new reform bill—submitted as the USA Freedom Act of 2015—would reauthorize certain aspects of that law while seeking to reform ways the government uses its spying capabilities. A similar reform bill was introduced last year in Congress, but ultimately did not gain enough support to pass.

"The bipartisan, bicameral USA Freedom Act of 2015 is the product of intense and careful negotiations between the House and Senate," said Sen. Patrick Leahy (D-Vt.) as he introduced the bill.

"If enacted, our bill will usher in the most significant reform to government surveillance authorities since the USA Patriot Act," said Leahy, adding that the law is designed to both "end the NSA's dragnet surveillance and protect Americans' privacy rights."

The new version of the USA Freedom Act will now compete with a parallel surveillance bill introduced earlier this month by Senate Majority Leader Mitch McConnell (Ky.) and Senate Intelligence Committee Chairman Richard Burr (N.C.), both Republicans. McConnell and Burr's bill would reauthorize the Patriot Act through the end of 2019 and entrench much of the domestic spying legal structures used by government agencies. This includes the re-authorization of Section 215, one of the most contentious provisions in the law that the NSA uses to conduct bulk phone records collection.

As the *Guardian*'s Spencer Ackerman explains in his most recent reporting, the USA Freedom Act remains a hard swallow for civil libertarians and privacy advocates because even though it sunsets Section 215 and includes other strong reforms, it also "contains several concessions to pro-surveillance legislators meant to facilitate its passage. Among them are expansions of temporary spying authorities to account for surveillance targets transiting into and out of the U.S., and an unrelated expansion of penalties for people convicted of lending 'material support' to terrorism."

As such, advocates of privacy and civil liberties offered mixed reactions to the bill on Tuesday, acknowledging the USA Freedom Act makes laudable attempts at reform in some key areas, while falling markedly short in others.

"When it comes to ending domestic bulk collection, this new version of the USA Freedom Act is clearly superior to the bill that passed the House of Representatives in 2014," said Harley Geiger, advocacy director and senior counsel at the Center for Democracy and Technology (CDT), in a statement. "The Patriot Act has been misappropriated for mass collection of Americans' sensitive information for too long, without any tangible benefit to security. Congress should not wait any longer to decisively rein in these egregious practices."

CDT acknowledged that comprehensive surveillance reform is still needed, but justified its support of the USA Freedom Act by saying its passage would represent significantly more progress than if the Patriot Act, and troubling provisions like Section 215, were given re-authorization without new constraints. As Greiger explained in a detailed Q&A about the bill on its website: "We'd certainly prefer to see the USA Freedom Act make far more reforms than it does. However, it is not an omnibus surveillance reform bill."

Jameel Jaffer, the deputy legal director of the American Civil Liberties Union (ACLU), however, expressed stronger dissatisfaction with the new version of the bill, telling the *Guardian* in a statement that it "doesn't go nearly far enough" to rein in mass surveillance or curb the worst abuses when it comes to government bulk data collection.

"While we appreciate the hard work of legislators like Senator Leahy, Representative Sensenbrenner, and Representative Conyers," said Jaffer, "this bill would make only incremental improvements, and at least one provision—the material-support provision—would be a step backwards. The disclosures of the last two years make clear that we need wholesale reform. Congress should let Section 215 sunset as it's scheduled to, and then it should turn to reforming the other surveillance authorities that have been used to justify bulk collection."

2

The US Patriot Act Threatens Library Patrons' Confidentiality

Dorotea Szkolar

Dorotea Szkolar is a graduate of Syracuse University's School of Information Studies. She works as a librarian and writes about technology use in libraries.

In this article, Dorotea Szkolar explains one of the most controversial sections of the US Patriot Act. Section 215 stipulates that any library patron's account can be monitored without a warrant in order to weed out domestic terrorism threats. According to Szkolar, this puts librarians in a tricky position of wanting to safeguard their patrons' rights while complying with the law and making sure the US government can adequately monitor any security threats. Libraries must have an official policy regarding the Patriot Act and make their policy known to patrons, especially because two presidents have upheld the act over the course of fifteen years. Since Szkolar's writing, the Patriot Act has expired and has been replaced with the USA Freedom Act. The most controversial aspect of Section 215— the bulk collection of data, notably used in collecting cell phone and library records—has been removed from the Freedom Act, although warrants are not needed for targeted collections, and Section 215 can continue to be used in "emergency" scenarios.

"The USA Patriot Act: Should Your Library Have an Official Policy?" Dorotea Szkolar, April 10, 2013. Reprinted by permission.

I volunteer as a reference librarian for an online text reference service on the weekends. At a recent staff meeting, the discussion came up on how to best implement an official policy regarding potential requests for patron reference records under the USA Patriot Act. For those unfamiliar with the topic, the USA Patriot Act was enacted by Congress in 2001 in response to the September 11 terrorist attacks on the World Trade Center and Pentagon. The intention of the act was to assist federal agents in better identifying and investigating possible terrorist threats by modifying preexisting surveillance law, especially concerning electronic communications, in non-emergency situations. Section 215 of the Patriot Act is commonly referred to as the "library provision" because it allows patron's library records to be accessed and monitored by law enforcement agencies without a traditional warrant.. The exact number of requests that have been made to libraries is unknown because of both gag orders and the general secrecy allotted to national security. Because a request under the Patriot Act violates a patron's confidentiality and librarians may be gagged from notifying the patron he or she is under investigation, it was a major concern for our reference service.

USA Patriot Act in Libraries: Summing of the Controversy

According to section 215 of the USA Patriot act, the FBI can request:

> Section. 501. (a)(1) The Director of the Federal Bureau of Investigation or a designee of the Director may make an application for an order requiring the production of any tangible things (including books, records, papers, documents and other items) for an investigation to protect against international terrorism or clandestine intelligence activities, provided that such investigation of a United States Person is not conducted solely upon the basis of activities protected by the first amendment to the constitution.

This means if a patron is under investigation by the FBI, the library is federally mandated to hand over a patron's library records.

Because of the broad language used in the act, these records may include: database records, circulation records, interlibrary loan records, reference interview records, and any records relating to electronic resources accessed on a library's computer. True, the patriot act specifically states any investigation cannot violate first amendment rights of U.S. citizens and must be approved by a recognized district court judge. An FBI agent cannot simply walk into a library and demand to see all of the private records without justification. However, many librarians and civil liberties advocates, including myself, believe this oversight is not enough. In 2008, for example, out of 2000 FBI warrant applications under the Patriot Act, only one was rejected by the FISA court. Critics argue that the FISA court merely rubber stamps applications for warrants.

Library groups continue to oppose the act. The ALA opposes the Patriot Act because of its threat to patron privacy and confidentially. It's official policy states: "any use of governmental power to suppress the free and open exchange of knowledge and information or to intimidate individuals exercising free inquiry" and the Patriot Act "presents danger to the constitutional rights and privacy rights of library users." States often have laws protecting the privacy of patron library records, and the professional ethics of librarianship require that patron confidentially and the right to access information without scrutiny be protected. However, the Patriot Act is federal and therefore legally trumps state/local laws and ethics. Academic librarians are especially concerned because they serve intellectual communities and facilitate access to a vast array of information, sometimes controversial, for legitimate scholarly research and academic discussion. While access to information may be for a legitimate scholarly endeavor, scholars may hesitate to access information if they fear potential persecution. The effect of self-censorship from fear or repercussion for all library patrons will negatively impact democracy in our country.

However, it is important to recognize law enforcement officials have an obligation to protect the United States of America and may have a legitimate reason to obtain patron records. It is known that the terrorist hijackers communicated through library computer terminals before the September 11 attacks. Specifically, Nawaf al-Hazmi and Khalid al-Midhar purchased and reviewed their airline reservations for their 9/11 flight at a New Jersey Library. The Department of Justice officially states that its investigators have no interest in the library habits of ordinary Americans, just protecting the United States.

You can find the full Uniting and Strengthening America by Providing Appropriate Tools Required to Intercept and Obstruct Terrorism Act here. *(Editor's note: You can find this act at the following web address: https://www.justice.gov/archive/ll/highlights .htm.)*

Patriot Act Policy

Libraries continue to adopt official policies to handle Patriot Act requests and make these available online for patrons to read. These policies do not impede law enforcement (nor would that be ethical to require of library staff) but rather ensure that only the necessary patrons records and information are accessed and the request be handled accordingly by library senior staff. Because of the Patriot Act, the ALA encourages libraries to only keep records of patron's information that are truly necessary: "American Library Association urges all libraries to adopt and implement patron privacy and record retention policies that affirm that "the collection of personally identifiable information should only be a matter of routine or policy when necessary for the fulfillment of the mission of the library"

In general, the official library policies I found online contain the following major components:

1. An explanation of what the Patriot Act is and how it allows law enforcements broad access to confidential patron information. Outside of the library world, most patrons are unaware of how significantly the Patriot Act impacts libraries and their personal information.

2. The libraries' official procedure for complying with Patriot Act requests. These often included an explanation of who would handle the request and the chain of command to be followed. In almost all policies, only the library director or higher official was authorized to fulfill Patriot Act requests. One academic library went so far as to guarantee only the director could handle FBI requests and would consult the legal team of the university administration before any records were supplied.

3. Many policies make it clear to patrons that federal law trumps any state or county laws enacted to protect library patron privacy and confidentiality laws. Additionally, the library officially opposes the Patriot Act but will comply with federal laws.

4. Finally, many policies listed the materials and services for which patron records with identifiable information are kept. In that way, patrons are aware of the information the library is keeping and therefore what is fair game to be investigated by the FBI under the Patriot Act.

In our post 9/11 world, the balance between civil liberties and privacy versus national security continues to play a prominent role in policy. While the Patriot Act is controversial, it has existed for over 10 years and been reauthorized by two different presidents. It appears the Patriot Act is here to stay and therefore libraries should expect at some point to be approached by the FBI under the Patriot Act. It would be best to have a policy and procedure in place when that happens.

3

Domestic Terrorists Are Waging War on Reproductive Rights

Anti-Defamation League

The Anti-Defamation League (ADL) is one of the United States' foremost civil rights organizations. Begun in 1913, the ADL fights against anti-Semitism and all other racial, economic, and social injustices.

Since 2012, the Anti-Defamation League has documented "America's forgotten terrorism"—increasing anti-abortion violence, often culminating in violent attacks on abortion clinics and providers. This is a worrisome form of "single issue" domestic terrorism, in which lone wolf perpetrators, who are often more difficult to track, are influenced by both social media and political messages. Finally, the ADL shows that this domestic terrorism is religious in nature and has developed largely from fundamentalist Christian views. Perhaps for this reason, the media have under-reported these attacks, which often are not covered beyond the local news.

B lack Friday" took on an altogether different meaning in Colorado Springs this past Thanksgiving weekend when, on November 27, a gunman embarked upon a deadly shooting spree at a local Planned Parenthood clinic. The shooter, Robert Lewis Dear, opened fire outside the clinic, then entered the building. As police arrived on the scene, Dear allegedly engaged them with gunfire, hitting several officers. Eventually, police launched an assault on the building to kill or capture the shooter, precipitating a firefight within the clinic. About five hours after the rampage began, Dear surrendered to police, who took him into custody.

The shootings took a deadly toll: killed were two civilians— Ke'Arre Stewart and Jennifer Markovsky—and a University of Colorado-Colorado Springs police officer, Garrett Swasey. Four other civilians and five more officers received non-fatal gunshot wounds.

At this early date, much remains unknown about the attack and the perpetrator's motives. Dear allegedly made the comment "no more baby parts" to police officers after his apprehension; this, plus the place and nature of the attack itself—at a Planned Parenthood clinic—suggests that an anti-abortion animus may well have been the motivation for the deadly attack. Both the mayor of Colorado Springs and the governor of Colorado subsequently labeled the rampage an act of terrorism.

The War on Reproductive Rights

If Dear's motive was indeed related to abortion, the Colorado Springs shooting spree represents the most deadly single act of anti-abortion violence in the United States. However, at the same time, it is only the latest in a long and troubling series of shootings, arsons, and other acts of violence directed against women's reproductive rights over the years. Many of these acts of anti-abortion violence have gone under-reported, not making it past the local news. In 2012, the Anti-Defamation League issued a report describing anti-abortion violence as "America's Forgotten Terrorism" and that is a label that is just as true today as it was three years ago—indeed, the list of violent anti-abortion acts has grown longer still.

With deadly attacks such as the Colorado Springs shootings or the 2009 assassination of Dr. George Tiller by an anti-abortion fanatic in Kansas, it is fair to refer to a war being waged on the reproductive rights of women across the United States.

This is a war that has several fronts. On the one hand, "mainstream" anti-abortion activists attempt to legislate and to regulate out of existence women's health clinics that offer abortions among their medical services. Accompanying this is a propaganda campaign designed to demonize abortion providers, a campaign exemplified recently by a series of videos released in 2015 by the anti-abortion Center for Medical Progress that purport to show Planned Parenthood officials selling "baby parts." The respected New England Journal of Medicine described the videos as a "campaign of misinformation."

It is important to acknowledge that this flood of "mainstream" demonization of the women's health centers that offer abortion services does play a role in abortion-related violence itself, providing an impetus to and justification for violent acts, even when the propaganda itself may not call for violence. When one analyzes acts of anti-abortion violence in the United States, a clear duality emerges. Many of the acts of anti-abortion violence are committed by hard-core, extremists, who often have been in the movement for years, and who frequently remain active in the movement even after being jailed for their acts. Such extremists need no further encouragement.

However, there is also a group of offenders that does not have that sort of prior history and record of commitment. Rather, they tend to be isolated and impressionable, sometimes with a history of mental or emotional problems, becoming receptive to the anti-abortion messages they hear around them to the point that they decide to target women's health providers with arson or worse. The growth of social media has made such messages even more common and accessible.

Those violent offenders represent the other front in the war against reproductive rights: a sustained campaign of harassment, stalking, threats and violence directed against women's health care clinics, as well as the doctors, nurses, employees and patrons of such facilities. For the most extreme anti-abortion activists, physically disrupting or halting the operations of clinics is a key goal, even if it means threatening, injuring or killing the people inside such clinics. For many of them, violence is indeed the solution. To give just one example, Michael Bray, a long-time anti-abortion extremist who spent time in prison for a series of clinic bombings in the 1980s, subsequently wrote and published the book *A Time To Kill,* which advocates the use of violence "in defense of the child in the womb." The book is currently sold on the website of The Army of God, a site devoted to portraying the perpetrators of anti-abortion violence and terrorism as heroes and martyrs and to advocating that others follow in their path.

Anti-Abortion Violence as Single Issue Terrorism

The most extreme tactics used by anti-abortion activists—including arsons and firebombings, bombings, and assassinations and shooting sprees—constitute terrorist acts. Anti-abortion violence is a form of "single issue terrorism," which is terrorism committed by extremists who are centered on a very specific and often narrow issue. Most single issue terrorist movements are actually the extreme wing of broader, more mainstream movements; that is certainly the case with anti-abortion terrorism. Many people in the United States oppose abortion, on various grounds, but only a minority is willing to commit extreme and violent acts to end the practice.

As a movement, anti-abortion extremists are extremely loosely organized—though well-networked. Organized, formal groups are typically shunned in favor of shadowy "conceptual" groups such as the so-called Army of God. The Army of God has no formal membership, structure, or leader; anyone can affiliate themselves with it simply by committing a violent act designed to further the anti-abortion cause.

A lot of anti-abortion extremist activity can be described as efforts intended to support the use of violence. Websites and documents created by anti-abortion extremists provide the addresses of clinics, as well as the names and personal information of doctors and others who work at such clinics. As with other extremist movements that use the same tactic, the hope is that individuals will be inspired to use such information in the commission of an act of violence. Some anti-abortion extremists have even provided instructions on constructing bombs and incendiary devices. Prominent anti-abortion extremist Dave Leach, for example, used his *Prayer & Action* magazine to distribute information about making plastic explosives and fertilizer bombs.

For those people who do commit violent acts, the movement acts as a support network, providing moral and other support for people convicted of acts of anti-abortion violence. Such prisoners—including notorious killers Paul Hill, Eric Rudolph, James Kopp and Scott Roeder, among others—are considered martyrs to the cause of ending abortions.

Many such extremists even continue their crusade from behind bars, hoping to influence others to follow their examples. Convicted murderer Scott Roeder, for example, has managed to provide the content for at least two anti-abortion videos on YouTube, one of which contained an implicit threat against a former employee of the physician Roeder murdered. Eric Rudolph, too, has provided written materials for the anti-abortion movement even while behind bars.

Because anti-abortion extremists constitute a mostly leaderless and structure-less movement, it is no surprise that much of the violence that emanates from the movement is lone wolf violence. What is perhaps surprising is the extent of the lone wolf violence coming from what is a relatively small movement—small in comparison to the major segments of the extreme right, such as white supremacist and anti-government extremist movements. A recently published study of lethal lone wolf violence in the United States by ADL Center on Extremism Director Mark Pitcavage observed that most lethal lone wolf violence was committed by right-wing extremists. Among them, anti-abortion extremists were among the most numerous, second only to white supremacists in number. One reason for this is the degree to which assassinations of physicians or clinic workers is condoned or even encouraged by anti-abortion extremists. With such encouragement, it is not surprising that self-appointed crusaders emerge from the shadows to do the deed.

At the less extreme end of the spectrum of anti-abortion violence are incidents of harassment, threats, and stalking. Such acts are intended to make life miserable for people associated with women's health clinics or to hinder or obstruct their operations.

One of the most notorious anti-abortion extremists who engaged in these sorts of activities was Clayton Lee Waagner, a violent criminal who became an anti-abortion crusader in the late 1990s. In the early 2000s, while a fugitive after an escape from jail, Waagner sent envelopes full of white powder to hundreds of clinics around the country. Notes enclosed in the envelopes claimed the powder was anthrax. As these incidents occurred shortly after the deadly anthrax letters of late 2001, the letters proved highly disruptive to health clinics, often forcing shutdowns and decontamination procedures. Waagner also send death threats to a variety of clinic employees. After his capture and conviction, Waagner received a 19-year prison sentence, but has continued anti-abortion activities from behind bars.

Waagner has many modern-day equivalents. In 2013, for example, a Kansas judge upheld a protection from stalking order against a Wichita anti-abortion activist, Mark Holick, for stalking and threatening the director of a local women's health clinic. He repeatedly showed up at her home and in her neighborhood, on one occasion with a sign that read "Where's Your Church?"—a reference to Kansas physician George Tiller, killed at his church by anti-abortion and anti-government extremist Scott Roeder in 2009. Anti-abortion extremist Angel Dillard targeted a Wichita physician, Mila Means, sending a letter to Means in which she claimed that people were constantly watching Means and that Means would have to check under her car every day, "because maybe today is the day someone places an explosive under it." Dillard subsequently claimed that her letter had been "divinely inspired."

Operation Save America, one of the more active organized anti-abortion extremist groups, embarked upon a campaign several years ago in which they placed "Wanted" posters in cities with clinics that allegedly provided abortion services—posters that listed addresses, even home addresses, of clinics and doctors.

Threats and harassment attempts have increased sharply in recent months after the release of the Center for Medical Progress videos in July 2015. According to the National Abortion Federation, harassment incidents rose sharply in the months that followed.

Some anti-abortion extremists are willing to do more than threaten and harass. They engage in violence against property, taking advantage of the fact that women's health clinics are permanent, immobile and mostly "soft" targets. This sort of violence can range from vandalism, petty or severe, up to more serious attacks such as bombings, firebombings, and arsons.

Many such incidents occur at night, suggesting that such attacks are primarily designed to target property, forcing the temporary or permanent shutdown of clinics by damaging them or even burning them to the ground. However, there are anti-abortion extremists who do target people themselves for attack, assaulting clinic workers or physicians or engaging in lethal violence. The Colorado Springs shooting spree may be an example of one such attack. The assassination of Dr. George Tiller by Scott Roeder certainly was. This attack, in which Roeder murdered Tiller while the doctor was serving as an usher at his church during Sunday services, was one of the key acts of terrorism that heralded a new resurgence of right-wing extremism that began in 2009 and continues to the present day.

There is one other fact about anti-abortion violence that is worth noting. As some of the below examples illustrate, a number of the extremists convicted for acts or attempts of anti-abortion violence over the years have also engaged in violence against other targets, notably Muslim and GLBT, but also sometimes Jewish, targets. These other acts of violence lend credence to the notion that anti-abortion violence in the United States is a form of distinctly

"Christian" terrorism, with many of these attacks stemming directly from the religious views of the extremists. Religious themes are a near constant within the world of anti-abortion extremism. As one judge characterized an anti-abortion extremist he was sentencing for attempted murder, "your religious certainty is so superior you thought you have the right to kill your intended victims."

Selected Incidents of Anti-Abortion Threats and Violence, 2006–2015

Note: This is only a partial list. Many anti-abortion incidents never even make it onto the media or into domestic terror databases.

- **Arson/Vandalism. Thousand Oaks, California, October 2015.** A Planned Parenthood clinic in the Newbury Park area of Thousand Oaks was victim to an arson attempt, only weeks after it suffered a vandalism attack. The building's sprinkler system put out the fire but in the process caused water damage.

- **Arson. Pullman, Washington, September 2015.** An arsonist caused substantial damage at a Planned Parenthood clinic in Pullman, Washington, forcing its closure for over a month.

- **Vandalism. Metairie, Louisiana, August 2015.** Prosecutors charged William Kennedy with criminal damage and a hate crime after he allegedly vandalized the Causeway Medical Clinic. Louisiana's hate crime law can be applied to someone who commits a crime against persons or property "because of actual or perceived membership or service in, or employment with, an organization."

- **Vandalism. Jackson, Mississippi, March 2015.** The Jackson Women's Health Organization building was the victim of serious vandalism.

- **Obstruction/Interference. Jackson, Mississippi, July 2014.** Three anti-abortion extremists were convicted of obstruction and interference with a lawful business after attempting to obstruct people's access to the Jackson Women's Health Organization. One of them, Chet Gallagher, had previously spent time in prison for using his status as a Las Vegas, Nevada, police officer, to gain access to a women's health clinic and destroy property inside.

- **Arson. Joplin, Missouri, October 2013.** Federal prosecutors charged Jedediah Stout with attempted arson of a building used in interstate commerce after twice attempting to set on fire a Planned Parenthood clinic in Joplin. After his arrest, Stout confessed to the arson attempts, and also confessed to having twice set fire to the mosque belonging to the Islamic Society of Joplin—the second time succeeding in completely destroying the building. As of October 2015, his case had not yet gone to trial.

- **Vandalism. Bloomington, Indiana, April 2013.** Bloomington police officers arrested Benjamin Curell of Elletsville on burglary and criminal mischief charges for using an axe to destroy windows and computers at a local Planned Parenthood clinic, causing extensive damage. In July 2014, Curell pleaded guilty to violating the federal Free Access to Clinic Entrances Act.

- **Arson. Atlanta and Marietta, Georgia, May 2012.** Blazes were set at two clinics in Georgia, one in Marietta and one in Atlanta, that provide abortion services. It is not clear if any arrests were ever made in these incidents, or if the incidents are connected.

- **Arson. Grand Chute, Wisconsin, April 2012.** Francis Grady set fire to a Planned Parenthood building in Grand Chute, causing damage but no injuries to people. He was convicted and, in February 2013, sentenced to 11 years in prison.

- **Firebombing. Pensacola, Florida, January 2012.** Bobby Joe Rogers used a Molotov cocktail to burn down a reproductive health clinic in Pensacola, Florida. That clinic had been repeatedly victimized with bombings and shootings since the 1980s. After pleading guilty, Rogers received a 10-year federal prison sentence.

- **Firebombing. McKinney, Texas, July 2011.** A Planned Parenthood clinic in McKinney, Texas, was firebombed with a Molotov cocktail-like incendiary device, causing moderate damage.

- **Assassination Plot. Madison, Wisconsin, May 2011.** Madison police uncovered a plot by Ralph Lang to assassinate physicians at a Planned Parenthood clinic in Madison. He was convicted of attempted first-degree intentional homicide in May 2013 and in August sentenced to 10 years in prison.

- **Bomb Plot. Greensboro, North Carolina, September 2010.** In a sting operation, federal agents arrested anti-abortion extremist Justin Carl Moose, on charges of providing information related to making a bomb or weapon of mass destruction to a person Moose thought was going to bomb a women's health clinic. On his Facebook page, Moose referred to himself as an "extremist radical fundamentalist" and argued that abortion should be fought "by any means necessary and at any cost." Moose pleaded guilty and received a 30-month federal prison sentence.

- **Firebombing. Madera, California, September 2010.** A Planned Parenthood clinic in Madera, California, was firebombed by someone claiming to be from the "American Nationalist Brotherhood." Vandalism at a local mosque was also claimed by the alleged group. An FBI investigation revealed that the culprit of both incidents was Donny Eugene Mower, a white supremacist. Mower pleaded guilty to federal counts of arson, damaging religious property and violating the Freedom of Access to Clinic Entrances Act. In 2012, he was sentenced to five years in prison.

- **Threats. Plano, Texas, April 2010.** FBI agents arrested Erlyndon J. Lo in Plano on allegations that he made death threats against the Southwestern Women's Surgery Center, charging him with using interstate commerce to communicate a threat to injure and threatening force to intimidate and interfere with clients and employees of a reproductive health service. He claimed that "my religious beliefs include the beliefs that an individual is alive at the moment of conception, abortion is murder and is the worst murder of all murders possible because these babies are completely defenseless, and I am entitled under my religious beliefs to use deadly force if necessary to save the innocent life of another." He was subsequently ruled incompetent to stand trial.

- **Threats. Spokane, Washington, June 2009.** Donald Hertz of Spokane, Washington, threatened the family of a Colorado physician whose office performed late term abortions. The threats came only weeks after the murder of another such physician, George Tiller, in Kansas. Hertz pleaded guilty and received a sentence of five years of probation.

- **Murder. Wichita, Kansas, May 2009.** Long-time anti-abortion and anti-government extremist Scott Roeder murdered physician George Tiller at Tiller's church in Wichita, Kansas. An unrepentant Roeder was convicted of first degree murder and aggravated assault and sentenced to life in prison.

- **Arson. Eureka, California, February 2008.** An arson occurred at a Planned Parenthood clinic in Eureka, California. A note taped to the front door made a reference to God and babies.

- **Arson. Albuquerque, New Mexico, December 2007.** On Christmas day, 2007, arsonists attacked two Planned Parenthood clinics in Albuquerque, damaging one with a Molotov cocktail and the other with vandalism. Earlier that month, on December 7, two men, Sergio Baca and Chad Altman, firebombed another New Mexico clinic because Baca's former girlfriend was going to have an abortion performed at that clinic. In 2009, they pleaded guilty to the crime, Baca receiving a 46-month federal sentence and Altman a 40-month sentence. They were also ordered to pay restitution of $796,531.92. It is not clear if anyone was ever arrested for either of the other two arsons.

- **Assassination. Amherst, New York, June 2007.** In 2007, anti-abortion assassin James Kopp, who murdered Dr. [Barnett] Slepian in New York in 1998, received a sentence of life imprisonment plus 10 years following a conviction on charges related to the 1998 killing. [Kopp] previously received a 25 years to life sentence on a second-degree murder charge in a New York court. Canadian authorities have also charged Kopp with the 1995 shooting of a physician in Ontario; he is suspected of possibly having shot a number of doctors in Canada in the 1990s. He has not been extradited to stand trial, however.

- **Bombing Attempt. Austin, Texas, April 2007.** Paul Ross Evans left a large bomb outside a women's health clinic in Austin, Texas, but it was discovered by an employee before detonating. Evans, who pleaded guilty to attempting to use a weapon of mass destruction, told a judge, "I never meant for anyone, except for the abortionists, to get hurt." He received a 40-year federal prison sentence.

- **Threats. Lancaster County, Pennsylvania, November 2006.** Pennsylvania State Police charged Mark Christian Stauffer with threatening to bomb a Planned Parenthood clinic in Lancaster. The disposition of the case is not known.

- **Arson. Davenport, Iowa, September 2006.** David McMenemy drove his car into the lobby of the Edgerton Women's Health Care Center in Davenport, Iowa, then used a Molotov cocktail to set the place on fire. He pleaded guilty to charges related to the attack in 2007 and received a five-year prison sentence.

- **Planned Bombing. Greenbelt, Maryland, June 2006.** Authorities arrested Robert Weiler for building a bomb to use to attack a local women's health clinic in Greenbelt, Maryland, as well as to shoot people inside. He was charged with possessing a pipe bomb and being a felon in possession of a firearm and subsequently pleaded guilty. He received a five-year sentence. In 2014, Prince George's County law enforcement officers arrested Weiler on charges of disorderly conduct and assault on a law enforcement officer outside a women's health clinic near College Park. The case was placed on Maryland's stet docket, which typically means that the charges will be dropped if certain conditions are met (such as community service, anger management classes, etc.).

- **Firebombing. Shreveport, Louisiana, January 2006.** Shreveport police charged Patricia Hughes and Jeremy Dunahoe with firebombing the Hope Medical Group for Women with a Molotov cocktail in December 2005. Luckily, the incendiary device was placed too far from the building and thus did little damage. Hughes pleaded guilty to the firebombing, while Dunahoe pleaded guilty to being an accessory. Hughes received a six-year sentence; Dunahoe a one-year sentence.

4

Eco-Terrorism Is Among the Greatest Current Threats to the Security of the United States

James F. Jarboe

James F. Jarboe is a special agent in the Federal Bureau of Investigation (FBI) who has been in charge of the FBI's Tampa Division. He has also worked as the domestic terrorism section chief in the Counterterrorism Division of the FBI and has frequently testified before Congress.

In this 2001 testimony before the US House of Representatives Resources Committee, James F. Jarboe states that special interest terrorism is becoming one of the most prevalent forms of domestic terrorism. In particular, environmental groups like the Sea Shepherd Conservation Society and the Animal Liberation Front (ALF) have increasingly depended on vandalism and other "terrorist activity" to forward their environmental objectives. According to Jarboe, this kind of "eco-terrorism" is a threat to the country's security and law enforcement around the country must be trained and able to prevent and investigate such terrorist activity. While the government often focuses on international terrorism in the wake of the September 11 terrorist attacks, eco-terrorism is a great threat to the country from within the United States.

G ood morning Chairman McInnis, Vice-Chairman Peterson, Congressman Inslee and Members of the Subcommittee. I am pleased to have the opportunity to appear before you and discuss

"The Threat of Eco-Terrorism," Federal Bureau of Investigation, February 12, 2002.

the threat posed by eco-terrorism, as well as the measures being taken by the FBI and our law enforcement partners to address this threat.

The FBI divides the terrorist threat facing the United States into two broad categories, international and domestic. International terrorism involves violent acts or acts dangerous to human life that are a violation of the criminal laws of the United States or any state, or that would be a criminal violation if committed within the jurisdiction of the United States or any state. Acts of international terrorism are intended to intimidate or coerce a civilian population, influence the policy of a government, or affect the conduct of a government. These acts transcend national boundaries in terms of the means by which they are accomplished, the persons they appear intended to intimidate, or the locale in which perpetrators operate.

Domestic terrorism is the unlawful use, or threatened use, of violence by a group or individual based and operating entirely within the United States (or its territories) without foreign direction, committed against persons or property to intimidate or coerce a government, the civilian population, or any segment thereof, in furtherance of political or social objectives.

During the past decade we have witnessed dramatic changes in the nature of the terrorist threat. In the 1990s, right-wing extremism overtook left-wing terrorism as the most dangerous domestic terrorist threat to the country. During the past several years, special interest extremism, as characterized by the Animal Liberation Front (ALF) and the Earth Liberation Front (ELF), has emerged as a serious terrorist threat. Generally, extremist groups engage in much activity that is protected by constitutional guarantees of free speech and assembly. Law enforcement becomes involved when the volatile talk of these groups transgresses into unlawful action. The FBI estimates that the ALF/ELF have committed more than 600 criminal acts in the United States since 1996, resulting in damages in excess of 43 million dollars.

Special interest terrorism differs from traditional right-wing and left-wing terrorism in that extremist special interest groups seek to resolve specific issues, rather than effect widespread political change. Special interest extremists continue to conduct acts of politically motivated violence to force segments of society, including the general public, to change attitudes about issues considered important to their causes. These groups occupy the extreme fringes of animal rights, pro-life, environmental, anti-nuclear, and other movements. Some special interest extremists—most notably within the animal rights and environmental movements—have turned increasingly toward vandalism and terrorist activity in attempts to further their causes.

Since 1977, when disaffected members of the ecological preservation group Greenpeace formed the Sea Shepherd Conservation Society and attacked commercial fishing operations by cutting drift nets, acts of "eco-terrorism" have occurred around the globe. The FBI defines eco-terrorism as the use or threatened use of violence of a criminal nature against innocent victims or property by an environmentally-oriented, subnational group for environmental-political reasons, or aimed at an audience beyond the target, often of a symbolic nature.

In recent years, the Animal Liberation Front (ALF) has become one of the most active extremist elements in the United States. Despite the destructive aspects of ALF's operations, its operational philosophy discourages acts that harm "any animal, human and nonhuman." Animal rights groups in the United States, including the ALF, have generally adhered to this mandate. The ALF, established in Great Britain in the mid-1970s, is a loosely organized movement committed to ending the abuse and exploitation of animals. The American branch of the ALF began its operations in the late 1970s. Individuals become members of the ALF not by filing paperwork or paying dues, but simply by engaging in "direct action" against companies or individuals who utilize animals for research or economic gain. "Direct action" generally occurs in the form of criminal activity to cause economic loss or to destroy the victims' company operations. The ALF activists have engaged in a steadily growing campaign of illegal activity against fur companies, mink farms, restaurants, and animal research laboratories.

Estimates of damage and destruction in the United States claimed by the ALF during the past ten years, as compiled by national organizations such as the Fur Commission and the National Association for Biomedical Research (NABR), put the fur industry and medical research losses at more than 45 million dollars. The ALF is considered a terrorist group, whose purpose is to bring about social and political change through the use of force and violence.

Disaffected environmentalists, in 1980, formed a radical group called "Earth First!" and engaged in a series of protests and civil disobedience events. In 1984, however, members introduced "tree spiking" (insertion of metal or ceramic spikes in trees in an effort to damage saws) as a tactic to thwart logging. In 1992, the ELF was founded in Brighton, England, by Earth First! members who refused to abandon criminal acts as a tactic when others wished to mainstream Earth First!. In 1993, the ELF was listed for the first time along with the ALF in a communique declaring solidarity in actions between the two groups. This unity continues today with a crossover of leadership and membership. It is not uncommon for the ALF and the ELF to post joint declarations of responsibility for criminal actions on their web-sites. In 1994, founders of the San Francisco branch of Earth First! published in The Earth First! Journal a recommendation that Earth First! mainstream itself in the United States, leaving criminal acts other than unlawful protests to the ELF.

The ELF advocates "monkeywrenching," a euphemism for acts of sabotage and property destruction against industries and other entities perceived to be damaging to the natural environment. "Monkeywrenching" includes tree spiking, arson, sabotage of logging or construction equipment, and other types of property destruction. Speeches given by Jonathan Paul and Craig Rosebraugh at the 1998 National Animal Rights Conference held at the University of Oregon, promoted the unity of both the ELF and the ALF movements. The ELF posted information on the ALF website until it began its own website in January 2001, and is listed in the same underground activist publications as the ALF.

The most destructive practice of the ALF/ELF is arson. The ALF/ELF members consistently use improvised incendiary devices equipped with crude but effective timing mechanisms. These incendiary devices are often constructed based upon instructions found on the ALF/ELF websites. The ALF/ELF criminal incidents often involve pre-activity surveillance and well-planned operations. Members are believed to engage in significant intelligence gathering against potential targets, including the review of industry/trade publications, photographic/video surveillance of potential targets, and posting details about potential targets on the internet.

The ALF and the ELF have jointly claimed credit for several raids including a November 1997 attack of the Bureau of Land Management wild horse corrals near Burns, Oregon, where arson destroyed the entire complex resulting in damages in excess of four hundred and fifty thousand dollars and the June 1998 arson attack of a U.S. Department of Agriculture Animal Damage Control Building near Olympia, Washington, in which damages exceeded two million dollars. The ELF claimed sole credit for the October 1998, arson of a Vail, Colorado, ski facility in which four ski lifts, a restaurant, a picnic facility and a utility building were destroyed. Damage exceeded $12 million. On 12/27/1998, the ELF claimed responsibility for the arson at the U.S. Forest Industries Office in Medford, Oregon, where damages exceeded five hundred thousand dollars. Other arsons in Oregon, New York, Washington, Michigan, and Indiana have been claimed by the ELF. Recently, the ELF has also claimed attacks on genetically engineered crops and trees. The ELF claims these attacks have totaled close to $40 million in damages.

The name of a group called the Coalition to Save the Preserves (CSP), surfaced in relation to a series of arsons that occurred in the Phoenix, Arizona, area. These arsons targeted several new homes under construction near the North Phoenix Mountain

Preserves. No direct connection was established between the CSP and ALF/ELF. However, the stated goal of CSP to stop development of previously undeveloped lands, is similar to that of the ELF. The property damage associated with the arsons has been estimated to be in excess of $5 million.

The FBI has developed a strong response to the threats posed by domestic and international terrorism. Between fiscal years 1993 and 2003, the number of Special Agents dedicated to the FBI's counterterrorism programs grew by approximately 224 percent to 1,669—nearly 16 percent of all FBI Special Agents. In recent years, the FBI has strengthened its counterterrorism program to enhance its abilities to carry out these objectives.

Cooperation among law enforcement agencies at all levels represents an important component of a comprehensive response to terrorism. This cooperation assumes its most tangible operational form in the Joint Terrorism Task Forces (JTTFs) that are established in 44 cities across the nation. These task forces are particularly well-suited to responding to terrorism because they combine the national and international investigative resources of the FBI with the street-level expertise of local law enforcement agencies. Given the success of the JTTF concept, the FBI has established 15 new JTTFs since the end of 1999. By the end of 2003 the FBI plans to have established JTTFs in each of its 56 field offices. By integrating the investigative abilities of the FBI and local law enforcement agencies, these task forces represent an effective response to the threats posed to U.S. communities by domestic and international terrorists.

The FBI and our law enforcement partners have made a number of arrests of individuals alleged to have perpetrated acts of eco-terrorism. Several of these individuals have been successfully prosecuted. Following the investigation of the Phoenix, Arizona, arsons noted earlier, Mark Warren Sands was indicted and arrested on 6/14/2001. On 11/07/2001, Sands pleaded guilty to ten counts of extortion and using fire in the commission of a federal felony.

In February 2001, teenagers Jared McIntyre, Matthew Rammelkamp, and George Mashkow all pleaded guilty, as adults, to title 18 U.S.C. 844(i), Arson, and 844(n), Arson Conspiracy. These charges pertain to a series of arsons and attempted arsons of new home construction sites in Long Island, New York. An adult, Connor Cash, was also arrested on February 15, 2001, and charged under the same federal statutes. Jared McIntrye stated that these acts were committed in sympathy of the ELF movement. The New York Joint Terrorism Task Force played a significant role in the arrest and prosecution of these individuals.

On 1/23/2001, Frank Ambrose was arrested by officers of the Department of Natural Resources with assistance from the Indianapolis JTTF, on a local warrant out of Monroe County Circuit Court, Bloomington, Indiana, charging Ambrose with timber spiking. Ambrose is suspected of involvement in the spiking of approximately 150 trees in Indiana state forests. The ELF claimed responsibility for these incidents.

On September 16, 1998, a federal grand jury in the Western District of Wisconsin indicted Peter Young and Justin Samuel for Hobbs Act violations as well as for animal enterprise terrorism. Samuel was apprehended in Belgium, and was subsequently extradited to the United States. On August 30, 2000, Samuel pleaded guilty to two counts of animal enterprise terrorism and was sentenced on November 3, 2000, to two years in prison, two years probation, and ordered to pay $364,106 in restitution. Samuel's prosecution arose out of his involvement in mink releases in Wisconsin in 1997. This incident was claimed by the ALF. The investigation and arrest of Justin Samuel were the result of a joint effort by federal, state, and local agencies.

On April 20, 1997, Douglas Joshua Ellerman turned himself in and admitted on videotape to purchasing, constructing, and transporting five pipe bombs to the scene of the March 11, 1997, arson at the Fur Breeders Agricultural co-op in Sandy, Utah. Ellerman also admitted setting fire to the facility. Ellerman was indicted on June 19, 1997 on 16 counts, and eventually pleaded guilty to three. He was sentenced to seven years in prison and restitution of approximately $750,000. Though this incident was not officially claimed by ALF, Ellerman indicated during an interview subsequent to his arrest that he was a member of ALF. This incident was investigated jointly by the FBI and the Bureau of Alcohol, Tobacco and Firearms (ATF).

Rodney Adam Coronado was convicted for his role in the February 2, 1992, arson at an animal research laboratory on the campus of Michigan State University. Damage estimates, according to public sources, approached $200,000 and included the destruction of research records. On July 3, 1995, Coronado pled guilty for his role in the arson and was sentenced to 57 months in federal prison, three years probation, and restitution of more than $2 million. This incident was claimed by ALF. The FBI, ATF, and the Michigan State University police played a significant role in the investigation, arrest, and prosecution.

Marc Leslie Davis, Margaret Katherine Millet, Marc Andre Baker, and Ilse Washington Asplund were all members of the self-proclaimed "Evan Mecham Eco-Terrorist International Conspiracy" (EMETIC). EMETIC was formed to engage in eco-terrorism against nuclear power plants and ski resorts in the southwestern United States. In November 1987, the group claimed responsibility for damage to a chairlift at the Fairfield Snow Bowl Ski Resort near Flagstaff, Arizona. Davis, Millet, and Baker were arrested in May 1989 on charges relating to the Fairfield Snow Bowl incident and planned incidents at the Central Arizona Project and Palo Verde nuclear generating stations in Arizona; the Diablo Canyon Nuclear Facility in California; and the Rocky Flats Nuclear Facility in Colorado. All pleaded guilty and were sentenced in September 1991. Davis was sentenced to six years in federal prison, and restitution to the Fairfield Snow Bowl Ski Resort in the amount of $19,821. Millet was sentenced to three years in federal prison, and restitution to Fairfield in the amount of $19,821. Baker was sentenced to one year in federal prison, five months probation, a $5,000 fine, and 100 hours of community service. Asplund was also charged and was sentenced to one year in federal prison, five years probation, a $2,000 fine, and 100 hours of community service.

Currently, more than 26 FBI field offices have pending investigations associated with ALF/ELF activities. Despite all of our efforts (increased resources allocated, JTTFs, successful arrests and prosecutions), law enforcement has a long way to go to adequately address the problem of eco-terrorism. Groups such as the ALF and the ELF present unique challenges. There is little if any hierarchal structure to such entities. Eco-terrorists are unlike traditional criminal enterprises which are often structured and organized.

The difficulty investigating such groups is demonstrated by the fact that law enforcement has thus far been unable to effect the arrests of anyone for some recent criminal activity directed at federal land managers or their offices. However, there are several ongoing investigations regarding such acts. Current investigations include the 10/14/2001 arson at the Bureau of Land Management Wild Horse and Burro Corral in Litchfield, California, the 7/20/2000 destruction of trees and damage to vehicles at the U.S. Forestry Science Laboratory in Rhinelander, Wisconsin, and the 11/29/1997 arson at the Bureau of Land Management Corral in Burns, Oregon.

Before closing, I would like to acknowledge the cooperation and assistance rendered by the U.S. Forest Service in investigating incidents of eco-terrorism. Specifically, I would like to recognize the assistance that the Forest Service is providing with regard to the ongoing investigation of the 7/20/2000 incident of vandalism and destruction that occurred at the U.S. Forestry Science Laboratory in Rhinelander, Wisconsin.

The FBI and all of our federal, state, and local law enforcement partners will continue to strive to address the difficult and unique challenges posed by eco-terrorists. Despite the recent focus on international terrorism, we remain fully cognizant of the full range of threats that confront the United States.

Chairman McInnis and Members of the Subcommittee, this concludes my prepared remarks. I would like to express appreciation for your concentration on the issue of eco-terrorism and I look forward to responding to any questions.

5

Extreme Animal Rights Activists Terrorize Biomedical Researchers

Pacific Standard Staff

Formerly Miller-McCune, Pacific Standard *is a bimonthly print and online magazine run by the Miller-McCune Center for Research Media and Public Policy.* Pacific Standard *focuses on progressive issues, including environmentalism, as they intersect with the behavioral and social sciences.*

According to the staff of Pacific Standard, *animal rights zealots use terrorism to provoke fear in the hearts of biomedical researchers. This leads to violence but also threatens biomedical research. In 2006, lobbying groups with members from the biomedical community helped pass the American Enterprise Terrorism Act (AETA). This act was quickly passed in the US Congress to clamp down on extreme animal activism, but many state that it has used too broad of a stroke and equates animal rights extremists with all supporters of animal rights, effectively equating animal rights activism with domestic terrorism.*

*T*his is the third of several stories exploring the contentious relationship between the scientific community, which insists animal research is essential to medical progresss, and the animal rights activists working to abolish animal experimentation. Earlier pieces included the effort to shift the debate from sidewalks to

"When Extreme Animal Rights Activists Attack," *Pacific Standard*, March 16, 2012.

courtrooms, and efforts to establish the "personhood" of species like apes and whales.

Daniel Andreas San Diego joined Osama bin Laden on the FBI's "Most Wanted Terrorists" watch list in 2009. Bin Laden is gone, but San Diego remains. Listed as "armed and dangerous," with a $250,000 price on his head, the Berkeley, California, native is only the second U.S. citizen to make this particular FBI list. He is 34, a vegan, and a skilled sailor. His tattoos depict burning, collapsing buildings. On his chest is a burning hillside coupled with the words, "It only takes a spark."

San Diego is an animal rights zealot. He is under federal indictment for allegedly igniting explosive devices outside two Northern California firms—biotechnology giant Chiron and homecare-product manufacturer Shaklee—in 2003. The FBI says a potentially deadly second explosive at Shaklee, strapped with nails and likely targeted at first responders, was defused.

Frankie Trull, founder and president of the Foundation for Biomedical Research, calls these "inexplicable, unforgiveable kinds of actions."

FBI assistant director Mike Heimbach calls them acts of terror, possibly meant to take lives, destroy property, and damage companies. The FBI has noted an uptick in violent rhetoric by animal activists and a shifting away from the code of nonviolence toward blatant threats and intimidation. Its website asserts that between 1979 and 2008, the Animal Liberation Front (ALF), the Earth Liberation Front, and other extremist groups have committed more than 2,000 criminal acts and caused $110 million in damages.

In a February 2011 *Nature* magazine poll, nearly a quarter of the animal research scientists who responded reported being affected by or knowing someone affected by animal rights activists. A little more than 15 percent had changed practices or direction as a result. Whether driven by fear or conscience, some large institutions are responding to calls for animal rights—this week, for example, the U.S. Environmental Protection Agency inked a deal with cosmetic maker L'Oreal that they hope brings them closer to one day using a computerized system to forecast a chemical's safety instead of using live animals.

Ultimately, as long as biomedical researchers continue experiments using animals, they're likely to have their own image problems in the war for hearts and minds.

In January, protesters waved signs asking the government to remove Harvard's animal-testing license for violations in Harvard-affiliated labs and to suspend animal testing there. Then, on March 1, the director of Harvard's New England Primate Research Center stepped down after the death of a fourth monkey in 21 months attributable to "human error."

In June 2010, a dead animal was found after being left in a cage being sanitized with water reaching 180 degrees Fahrenheit. The facility said it died before entering the washer. Research is currently suspended at the center, which has more than 1,700 monkeys and has received 19 citations from the USDA for Animal Welfare Act violations in three years.

Daniel Andreas San Diego's gripe with Chiron and Shaklee, authorities believe, was that both companies apparently did business with Huntingdon Life Sciences, one of the world's largest contract research organizations, with operations in the United Kingdom, United States, and Japan. It provides animal-testing facilities and services to clients in such industries as pharmaceuticals, food, and chemicals.

Huntingdon has long aroused the ire of moderates as well as extremists. Since 1989, disturbing undercover footage—from showing a beagle pup being punched in the face to a live monkey being dissected apparently while conscious—has emerged from various undercover investigations. In 2001, a Huntingdon executive in the U.K. was severely beaten by three masked extremists bearing bats.

The FBI believes San Diego has ties to Stop Huntingdon Animal Cruelty and ALF—two groups blamed for some of the most dangerous criminal acts in the name of animal liberation. ALF is an amorphous organization with autonomous underground cells of outliers. San Diego has been described as a "lone wolf," Stop Huntingdon Animal Cruelty and the ALF as "leaderless resistance."

ALF's website says it "has historically been opposed to violence against any living being, though other groups and activists do not observe this limitation." Defending illegal actions like property destruction, it says: "Members of the ALF and other underground organizations feel that in order to truly liberate animals, the unjust laws that allow their exploitation must be broken."

The broader cause was surely not helped, however, by former trauma surgeon and ALF-affiliate Jerry Vlasak's infamous words during a Senate committee hearing in 2005. Vlasak, a medical doctor, opined that killing scientists and biomedical researchers who won't stop hurting animals can be, when nothing else will work, a "morally justifiable solution."

According to a tally at the website Idealist.org, there are 1,626 nonprofit animal-related groups in the U.S. For armchair sympathizers and peaceable activists and protesters alike, the handiwork of the fanatical minority is a liability.

"All we need is one death or serious injury," says Chris DeRose, Last Chance for Animals president and founder, "and it would set the movement back decades."

In a sense, zealots like Vlasak serve the biomedical research community as useful enemies, handing it compelling justifications for locked laboratory doors and research secrecy. Whether that bunker mentality works is another question: In the U.K., increased transparency has been seen as calming animal rights actions (in tandem with tougher laws and moderates' revulsion at the worst extremist acts). According to TheEconomist last October, while legal protests against U.K. animal-testing facilities are up, illegal attacks are currently down.

Stop Huntingdon Animal Cruelty (SHAC) was founded in Britain in 1999 to try to shut down its namesake's laboratories. It targeted firms doing business with Huntingdon or with financial ties to the organization; the biotech industry fought back, telling the British government that the U.K. drug industry would boycott those who caved in to SHAC.

In May 2004, seven activists were brought up on federal criminal charges for running SHAC's U.S. website. In hopes of shutting Huntingdon's New Jersey facility, the website routinely posted news supporting illegal acts like vandalism and releasing animals from laboratories alongside news of legal actions.

In 2006, six of the activists received one to six years in prison for crimes centered on encouraging others to harass and intimidate Huntingdon employees.

Theirs were the first convictions using 1992's Animal Enterprise Protection Act, which made stealing from or causing damage or property loss to an "animal enterprise" a criminal activity. In November 2006, the rarely used law was replaced by the Animal Enterprise Terrorism Act, or AETA.

At least two heavy-hitting lobbying groups with members in biomedical research and other industries with a financial stake in these issues were instrumental in the passage of the AETA. *Marie Claire* reported in 2011 that the American Legislative Exchange Council drafted the law working closely with members of Congress and that the group's members included 2,400 state lawmakers and 80 members of Congress. The National Association for Biomedical Research also rallied behind the AETA, creating the group Animal Enterprise Protection Coalition.

Will Potter, a journalist, civil rights and domestic terrorism expert and the author of *Green Is the New Red: An Insider's Account of a Social Movement Under Siege*, says the biotech nonprofits lobbied with the support of corporations like Pfizer, Wyeth, Glaxo Smith Kline, The National Cattlemen's Beef Association, the Fur Farmers, which he identifies as "the driving force on this." Other groups supporting the AETA ranged from the Pet Food Institute, the American Psychological Association, the American Veal Association, and the American Brain Coalition.

Potter recalls the law whizzing through Congress, and believes few realized how insidious it was until it was too late. Rep. Dennis

Kucinich, D-Ohio, sounded a lonely voice of dissent in Congress. "The bill was written to have a chilling effect on a specific type of protest," he warned. "We have to be very careful of painting everyone with the broad brush of terrorism."

Many civil libertarians and First Amendment experts argue it equates protest with terrorism and stifles protected speech and the right to assemble. Potter believes the AETA is part of a larger campaign to demonize all supporters of animal rights, not only the movement's radicals.

Attorney Odette Wilkens is the founder of The Equal Justice Alliance, a coalition of more than 200 social justice and animal protection organizations that, along with the Center for Constitutional Rights, the Civil Liberties Defense Center and others, is working to repeal the AETA.

"AETA stands the First Amendment on its head," she says. "Compared to other groups who are violent and murdered many people on a premeditated basis, such as anti-abortionists and white supremacists, animal activists have been singled out as the No. 1 domestic terrorism threat, even though they have never killed a single person." She says the AETA criminalizes protected speech.

"AETA is clear," Wilkens argues. "If you 'interfere' with an animal enterprise and cause it profit loss, you are a terrorist."

The law specifically says that "economic damage … does not include any lawful economic disruption (including a lawful boycott) that results from lawful public, governmental, or business reaction to the disclosure of information about an animal enterprise." It also says nothing in it "shall be construed to prohibit any expressive conduct (including peaceful picketing or other peaceful demonstration) protected from legal prohibition by the First Amendment to the Constitution."

But opponents such as the New York City Bar say its vagueness and broadness essentially render these protections worthless

Where to draw a line between protected acts and "interference" is unsettled, and opponents of the law say it creates a chilling effect on the kinds of undercover investigations that historically have been important in uncovering egregious activities in research facilities and livestock operations. Other laws bubbling up at the state level to heighten it include so-called "ag-gag" laws that criminalize gaining access to livestock operations under false or undercover pretenses to document abuses. Iowa's governor signed the first such law in the nation last week, and Utah looks set to soon have the second.

Pushes for tougher ALEC-inspired legislation at the state level led the National Lawyers Guild to argue this allows "private interests to redefine what it means to be an activist, a criminal, and a terrorist under United States law."

In December, the Center for Constitutional Rights filed a federal lawsuit, *Blum v. Holder*, in Massachusetts on behalf of five longtime activists who want the AETA struck down as unconstitutional and a violation of the First Amendment.

The first indictments under AETA came in March 2009. Four activists were accused of being involved in protests that included a February 2008 demonstration outside a UC Santa Cruz cancer researcher's home. They allegedly wore masks, shook the researcher's door, and frightened her two young children before being chased away; the incident was described as an attempted home invasion. One activist allegedly also hit the researcher's husband with an object in a scuffle. The four, who could have faced 10-year sentences, saw their cases dismissed in July 2010 for being too vague and non-specific.

Other UC-related protest incidents include trespassing on a UC Berkeley professor's front yard and accusing him of being a murderer. And defamatory comments have been chalked on public sidewalks outside researchers' residences.

More serious incidents have taken place.

On March 7, 2009, an early-morning blast woke David Jentsch, a UCLA psychologist and neuroscientist conducting schizophrenia, amphetamine, and addiction research on rodents and vervet monkeys. Jentsch's Volvo had been firebombed. The Animal Liberation Brigade took responsibility. In November 2010,

Jentsch received a razor blade-filled package and a note threatening to slash his throat from another extremist group calling itself the Justice Department,.

This February, Jentsch was one of three UCLA scientists honored by the American Association for the Advancement of Science for bravery in the face of ongoing intimidation and for strongly defending the importance of animals in research. Jentsch maintained that continuing his research was a moral obligation. And inspired by the U.K. pro-research group Pro-Test, in 2009 he and others of like mind formed Pro-Test for Science. Its principle: "science, reasoned discourse and the belief that life-saving medical research must continue without violence and harassment from misguided activists."

Gruesome images periodically emerge—a primate at Cornell whose lungs essentially burst during a 2009 surgery, baboons that inspectors found at Yale in 2010 with blisters and burns from heating pads, 32 monkeys cooked alive at a Reno, Nevada, facility of when a heater was left on—confirming activists' worst suspicions that even with the Animal Welfare Act and USDA inspections and regulations, the system can and does fail, riling activists and inciting extremists.

Veterinarian Robert Dysko, president of the American Association for Laboratory Animal Science and the associate director of the University of Michigan's Unit for Laboratory Animal Medicine, is not insensitive to these issues.

"I become concerned when I see the abuses," he admits, "and certainly there has been some footage that has troubled me." But he cautions against a rush to judgment noting that the lay public may not always realize that animals seen in awkward-looking positions are anesthetized.

"Are there things in some of this footage that bother me? Yes. I'm not going to pretend that there aren't things that are of concern," Dysko says. "But are there things in there that are being shown and people are horrified by it that are actually OK in the scientific community? Yes."

The metal halos worn by human patients with skeletal conditions requiring extensive bone manipulation were almost all developed using animals. "You take a picture of the animal with that on it," says Dysko, "a person would say, 'That's absolutely horrible.'" Dysko hopes people will remember that animals also benefit from medical advances, with the pacemaker "a classic example of developed in animals for people, back in use in animals."

"There is no excuse for institutions that house animal research—including most research universities—not to have vigorous and well-defined programs to explain what goes on within their walls," says the science magazine *Nature*. "They should also discuss their strategies to replace animals with more sophisticated research tools, refine research practice, and reduce the overall number of animals used. If they have no such strategies, institutions should develop them as a priority."

When Oregon Health and Science University's P. Michael Conn, recalls his harassment, he says he never heard it mentioned "that my institution is fully accredited and in compliance with all federal and state laws." The National Primate Research Center there—Conn is its director of the Office of Research Advocacy—is one of eight federally sponsored primate research centers housing almost 4,000 nonhuman primates.

In 2002, he told a hearing of the FBI's Joint Terrorism Task Force that PETA had created a webpage to disparage him and to "recruit correspondents to harass me with emails and letters. The site focused not on my own scientific investigations but on the fact that I work for an institution that conducts animal research." Over the years, Oregon Health and Science University has repeatedly been accused of maltreating research animals. The USDA has cited it for Animal Welfare Act violations and did so after complaints by People for the Ethical Treatment of Animals in 2008. USDA inspections following more PETA allegations in 2010, however, came up clean.

But animal advocates generally are not reassured by what many view as a lax system of accreditation and inadequate oversight.

According to New England's Anti-Vivisection Society website, approximately 150 inspectors oversee 12,000 licensed facilities. Animal advocates want greater transparency.

For example, there are no reliable population figures for research animals in the United States since 95 percent are purpose-bred rodents. Not covered or protected by the Animal Welfare Act, they are not counted. And it's not much clearer for more charismatic animals judging by annual reports from the USDA's Animal and Plant Health Inspection Service (APHIS). Initially, the 2008 and 2009 reports pleased the Humane Society of the United States because they offered the public a more accurate picture by including the numbers for a population of animals the USDA says "have been bred, conditioned, and/or held for use in research, but not yet used."

The 2009 grand total was 1,131,076 animals, including 146,417 nonhuman primates. But in February 2011, the USDA amended those numbers to a reduced total of 979,772 animals including 70,444 primates. The difference? The 151,434 animals and 53,941 primates "not yet used," while still noted within the reports, were again removed from the grand total. David Sacks, the USDA/APHIS public affairs officer, explained via email that including them was a mistake now corrected.

But Kathleen Conlee, director of program management for animal research issues for the Humane Society of the United States (HSUS), was disappointed, saying the lower numbers mislead the public: "Anyone would look at that table and think those numbers account for all animals in labs. I would say that breeding should count as being 'used.' Particularly given my experience working at a primate breeding facility, it wasn't like those animals lived a life free of stress by any means."

The biomedical research community's response to criticism is commonly to say that laboratories are strictly regulated.

But with oversight limited, to a large extent, facilities must police themselves.

The NIH calls each facility's Institutional Animal Care and Use Committee (IACUC) "the cornerstone" to its plan to ensure "the highest standards for animal use." These review bodies oversee all research and are mandatory in institutions receiving federal research dollars. But they are loaded with researchers. Small facilities' committees have at least five members and must include a veterinarian and one "public member" with no ties to the facility.

Robert Dysko understands if IACUCs don't allay outsiders' concerns, but he believes in the system. "Now, whether it works 100 percent of the time, yeah, I can't say that, and I really wouldn't say that, but it does work," he says. "Everyone accepts their responsibility pretty solidly."

Dysko's Michigan facility's IACUC comprises 16 to 18 people: two citizen members plus a third non-scientist. Citizen members are usually found by word of mouth and do have a voice at Michigan, he says. Generally, IACUC members' identities are closely guarded for security reasons; the Animal Legal Defense Fund's Joyce Tischler wishes at least some were drawn from the animal protection community. "So we scratch our heads," she says, "and we get cynical and suspicious and say, 'Well, what are you hiding?'"

Animal protection laws fall far short for animal welfare activists' liking anyway. The law, for example, doesn't forbid any experiment, albeit painful or unnecessary or frivolous-sounding. And painkillers are not given for all procedures. Also, even when viable alternatives to animals are available, the law doesn't require that they're used, only that they be considered, with reasons for not using them documented.

The Physicians Committee for Responsible Medicine reports in a position paper that even routine laboratory procedures and typical laboratory experiments that appear minimally invasive can be highly stressful for animals. And stressed animals, whether rodents or far larger species, compromise results. "Research on immune function, endocrine and cardiovascular disorders, neoplasms, developmental defects, and psychological phenomena," it says, "are particularly vulnerable to stress effects." Frankie Trull of the Foundation for Biomedical Research concurs that "not on a moral or ethical standpoint but from a pure scientific standpoint, sound data is critical to the viability of a study."

Matt Rossell, campaigns director of Animal Defenders International, was a "psychological well-being" primate technician at Oregon Health and Science University from 1998 to 2000. Experienced in working with depressed or agitated self-injuring monkeys, he asks: "How can you get good data from a monkey that's so stressed out?" Rossell began secretly filming their condition and living conditions at OHSU before leaving his job.

The EPA-L'Oreal partnership is a step forward. But as Martin Stephens, HSUS's vice president of animal research issues, says, animal studies will remain part of the approval process for drugs until the FDA is convinced that better methods are available. "There is near consensus that the current testing scheme is broken for pharmaceuticals," he says. "New, better methods are on the way."

Ultimately, the best hope for real peace and unity likely lies in his suggestion that the FDA "invest heavily in the new tools and approaches so that they can replace animal methods sooner rather than later."

6

Dealing with Domestic Terrorism Is a Catch-22

David Alpher

David Alpher, PhD, is an adjunct professor at the School for Conflict Analysis and Resolution at George Mason University. He has spent many years applying conflict resolution theory and methodology to international development work in Iraq, Israel, Palestine, and other countries.

Written during the presidential primaries in 2016 and immediately following the occupation of the Malheur National Wildlife Refuge by the radical Bundy brothers, this article explores how violent extremist groups have become more active in the United States in recent years. As seen in the occupation of Malheur, in which an armed group led by Ammon Bundy took over the land to protest the US government's legitimacy, these right-wing radical groups are often fueled by increasing governmental action. Thus, the US government finds itself in a catch-22: more governmental action can lead to increased tension and violence, while complacence will allow such violent direct action to continue in the future. According to the author, this is compounded by the fact that extreme factions have been adopted into the Republican Party's mainstream.

After a weeks-long standoff with federal and Oregon state police, 16 members of the Malheur National Wildlife Refuge occupation have been arrested, one wounded and another killed. The occupation's leaders, Ammon and Ryan Bundy, are among those in custody.

Although some of the foot soldiers remain on federal land, the occupation's end is inevitable. But the end of the siege will do nothing to reduce the increasing threat from America's radical right wing.

The official response to both this current takeover and last summer's standoff at the Bundy ranch in Nevada has been subdued. Given that in both cases the radicals were heavily armed and threatening to kill anyone who tried to arrest them, the fact that only one militant has lost his life is startling.

I have spent 14 years studying terrorism and extremism in conflict. The militants in Malheur aren't, in my view, currently terrorists, but groups like theirs have performed acts of domestic terrorism in the past. I believe the country's leadership needs to work quickly to stop that from happening again.

"Act or do nothing" is a false choice

Restraint is certainly preferable to the violence of the federal actions at the compound of Randy Weaver in Ruby Ridge, Idaho and the Branch Davidian cult's compound in Waco, Texas in 1992 and 1993, respectively. Each of those cases began as investigations into the sale or possession of illegal firearms and escalated into sieges involving multiple agencies.

In Waco, the siege ended with a full-scale assault on the compound, four federal agents killed and 16 wounded. Eighty-two members of the Branch Davidians were killed, including 17 children.

Ruby Ridge ended with a U.S. marshall killed along with two members of the Weaver household, and two more wounded. One of the dead was Weaver's 14-year-old son, and one of the wounded was his pregnant wife.

Two years later, Timothy McVeigh bombed the Murrah Building in Oklahoma City, killling 168 and injuring more than 600 others, in retaliation for Waco and Ruby Ridge.

The comparative restraint demonstrated recently at the Bundy ranch and Malheur suggests the government has taken a clear lesson to heart: there are more militants out there, and they are watching.

Double Standard

Unfortunately there is also legitimate protest that had these armed occupiers been anything but white, we'd likely have seen far less restraint.

In 1985, Philadelphia police responded to the occupation of a house by the black power group MOVE by dropping a firebomb that ultimately killed 11 people and left another 250 homeless. In 1973, the occupation of Wounded Knee by the American Indian Movement resulted in federal troops called up on American soil and ended with two dead and 15 wounded. More recently, we saw a militarized police reaction to a series of racial protests following the killing of Michael Brown in Ferguson, Missouri.

Even noting the double standard, the degree of restraint shown in Malheur is still admirable. The current U.S. domestic strategy for countering violent extremism correctly recognizes that while violent or armed responses are occasionally needed, they are usually more effective at driving further violence than at ending it. Threat reduction should focus on preventing the cause of radicalization rather than attempting to crush the symptom. That means focusing on inclusive governance, ending social marginalization and focusing on community policing instead of violent reaction.

In the current political climate, however, restraint also has a dangerous edge. It gives the impression of leaving the field to emboldened extremists, who are now claiming victory. That's a dangerous precedent, especially as such groups are showing a shift toward direct action that the U.S. hasn't seen for a long time.

Right-wing extremists are on the rise domestically, becoming more active and far bolder than they used to be.

The Diversity Effect

Between President Obama's election in 2008 and 2012, the Southern Poverty Law Center reports that the number of right-wing extremist groups operating in the U.S. increased by over 800 percent. While we've seen a slight decrease over the past year, the U.S. now faces a perfect storm of conditions for resurgent growth.

As the tone of the presidential election has proven, the prevailing American emotion is anger. Mistrust of government is at record high levels, along with several beliefs that make the problem worse.

First is the belief among extremists that the government is not simply untrustworthy but actually an enemy.

Second is the belief that anyone who supports the other side is the enemy as well.

In addition, the perception by the Christian right wing is that they are fundamentally threatened with extinction by changing American demographics.

And the double standard in federal response to extremism on the left and right is driving an increase in tension on the nonwhite side as well.

It Could Get Worse

All of this amounts to fertile ground for growing extremists. The presidential election is only adding fuel to the fire.

A Hillary Clinton victory would be seen by right-wing radicals as entrenching the same liberal sentiments that extremist organizations like the Oath Keepers—involved at both the Bundy ranch and Malheur—already hold up as the enemy. Bernie Sanders calling himself a socialist makes him seem even more alien.

On the Republican side, GOP candidates and officeholders alike have failed to condemn the occupiers. At least one—Representative Andy Holt of Tennessee—has made explicit statements of support.

Not only does this legitimize the right wing, but it also sends an ominous message to non-Christian and nonwhite America.

The GOP as a whole has become more radical from top to bottom—sto the point where an article written in bipartisan collaboration between Thomas Mann and Norman Ornstein (the former with the liberal Brookings Institution, the latter with the conservative American Enterprise Institute) labeled the entire party an "insurgent outlier" in American politics.

The party faces a growing divide between its white, Christian base and a population that bears it less resemblance by the year. They have sought to bridge that divide by inviting more and more of their own fringe to the table, to the point where extremist "sovereign citizens" and "patriot militias" now find themselves close to the party's mainstream. Nativist xenophobia coming from the GOP presidential candidates lends an air of legitimacy to language that should have been universally denounced as political extremism long ago.

All of this means that the U.S. government finds itself in a catch-22: becoming more assertive, having previously backed down, is likely to fuel aggression from right-wing radicals. On the other hand, if the government doesn't become more aggressive, the trend toward direct action will continue.

Victory means navigating the narrow ground between violence and capitulation. It means avoiding the double standard and applying consistent restraint to everyone, regardless of color or religion. The perfect storm can still be averted, but course corrections need to be set in motion as soon as possible.

There is little more dangerous than an extremist who feels betrayed, as Timothy McVeigh taught us.

7

The Sovereign Citizens Movement May Be the Biggest Domestic Terrorist Threat in the United States

Bill Berkowitz

Bill Berkowitz is a freelance writer based in Oakland, California, who covers conservative movements. He is the cofounder of the DataCenter, a research library for social and political activists, and won the Special Journalism Award in 2005 from the Before Columbus Foundation.

In recent years, the Sovereign Citizens movement has become the biggest threat to the United States, beating out militias, environmental extremists, and animal rights extremists. The Sovereign Citizens movement developed early in President Barack Obama's presidency and is firmly rooted in racist beliefs, although members of the movement may not be fully aware of this. Members hold "bizarre" anti-government beliefs and often try to block US courts; fight against paying taxes; and may even resort to violence against government officials. They have gained more traction due to the recent economic crisis and must be considered a major threat to American security, even considering the rise of international terrorist groups like the Islamic State of Iraq and Syria (ISIS).

In late-September, Thomas David Deegan, a man described by authorities as an anti-government sovereign citizen, was arrested

"Sovereign Citizens' Movement May Be Biggest Domestic Terrorist Threat," Bill Berkowitz, October 6, 2015, ©Truthout.org. Reprinted with permission.

and accused "of plotting to overthrow the state government in West Virginia, hoping to establish a prototype for extremists to follow in other states," the Southern Poverty Law Center reported. At the same time, the federal Department of Housing and Urban Development, issued a report "advising contractors, property inspectors, Section 8 housing administrators and Realtors how to recognize antigovernment sovereign citizens occupying vacant properties or using false deeds to support leasing."

In just seven years, the Sovereign Citizen movement, a movement that most Americans know little about, has vaulted to the top of the list of terrorist threats to the homeland according to a survey of law enforcement officials. Sovereign citizens has leaped over such better-known entities as local militias/patriots, environmental extremists, animal rights extremists, racist skinheads, neo-Nazis, and Islamic extremists, to grab the number one spot in a survey conducted by the National Consortium for the Study of Terrorism and Responses to Terrorism.

According to vox.com's Zack Beauchamp, "In a 2014 survey, the National Consortium for the Study of Terrorism and Responses to Terrorism (START) surveyed hundreds of law enforcement personnel at the state and local level, all of whom had training in intelligence gathering or counterterrorism. They were presented with a list of radical groups and asked to rate, on a scale of 1 to 4, how much they agreed that this group posed a terrorist threat to the US."

Given that the report was done last year before ISIS started grabbing headlines and before several mass shootings by homegrown white males, the list might look different today.

Nevertheless, as Beauchamp noted in a late August piece for Vox, it is more than worthwhile trying to get a handle on what the sovereign citizen movement is all about.

According to a Southern Poverty Law Center profile of the Sovereign Citizens Movement, "adherents hold truly bizarre, complex antigovernment beliefs, ... believ[ing] that they get to decide which laws to obey and which to ignore, and they don't think they should have to pay taxes."

They are "clogging up the courts with indecipherable filings" and have been responsible for a number of "acts of deadly violence, usually directed against government officials."

"Rooted in racism," the SPLC points out, "most sovereigns, many of whom are African American, are" likely to be "unaware of their beliefs' origins." When the movement started in the early 1980s, it "attracted white supremacists and anti-Semites, mainly because sovereign theories originated in groups that saw Jews as working behind the scenes to manipulate financial institutions and control the government.

"Most early sovereigns, and some of those who are still on the scene, believed that being white was a prerequisite to becoming a sovereign citizen. They argued that the 14th Amendment to the Constitution, which guaranteed citizenship to African Americans and everyone else born on U.S. soil, also made black Americans permanently subject to federal and state governments, unlike themselves."

Sovereigns believe that the founding fathers set up a "legal system the sovereigns refer to as 'common law'—was secretly replaced by a new government system based on admiralty law, the law of the sea and international commerce. Under common law, or so they believe, the sovereigns would be free men. Under admiralty law, they are slaves, and secret government forces have a vested interest in keeping them that way."

The movement "stake their lives and livelihoods on the idea that judges around the country know all about this hidden government takeover but are denying the sovereigns' motions and filings out of treasonous loyalty to hidden and malevolent government forces."

The number of sovereign citizens is unclear as "there is no central leadership and no organized group that members can join," SPLC points out. Those interested in the movement often attend seminars, go online and visit the many websites and chat-rooms open to sovereign citizens. After this rather abbreviated course of instruction, some are moved to "testing sovereign ideology with small offenses such as driving without a license, while others proceed directly to taking on the IRS as tax protesters."

Interestingly, sovereign citizens use "paper" as their primary weapon. A simple offense can result in a sovereign citizen filing a barrel full of paperwork regardless of the severity of the offense. "The size of the documents is an issue, but so is the nonsensical language the documents are written in. They have a kind of special sovereign code language that judges, lawyers and other court staff simply can't understand (nor can most non-sovereigns)," SPLC points out.

In economic hard times, i.e. the past decade and a half, the movement attracted many people in desperate financial straits. "Others are intrigued by the notions of easy money and living a lawless life, free from unpleasant consequences."

The movement has also seen its share of violent confrontations.

According to the SPLC report, "In 1995 in Ohio, a sovereign named Michael Hill pulled a gun on an officer during a traffic stop. Hill was killed. In 1997, New Hampshire extremist Carl Drega shot dead two officers and two civilians, and wounded another three officers before being killed himself. In that same year in Idaho, when brothers Doug and Craig Broderick were pulled over for failing to signal, they killed one officer and wounded another before being killed themselves in a violent gun battle. In December 2003, members of the Bixby family, who lived outside of Abbeville, S.C., killed two law enforcement officers in a dispute over a small sliver of land next to their home. And in May 2010, Jerry and Joseph Kane, a father and son sovereign team, shot to death two West Memphis, Ark., police officers who had pulled them over in a routine traffic stop. Later that day, the Kanes were killed in a fierce shootout with police that wounded two other officers."

In light of the recent growth of ISIS, it remains to be seen if the Sovereign Citizen Movement will continue to be seen by law enforcement officials as America's number one terrorist threat. Stay tuned.

8

Sovereign Citizens Engage in a Wide Range of Terrorist Activity and Must Be Stopped

Charles Loeser

Charles Loeser received his Juris Doctor from the University of North Carolina School of Law. He is currently an associate at Cravath, Swaine & Moore.

"Sovereign citizen" is a catchall term that describes a variety of people who distrust and dislike the US government and share a core set of common beliefs—most important, the belief that the government is illegitimate. Growing out of the militia movement and tax protesters, the Sovereign Citizens movement has developed in recent years to become a major threat to US governance. Sovereign citizens typically engage in tactics such as "paper terrorism," in which they falsify government documents and file fraudulent lawsuits, although they also have engaged in terror and murder. In this excerpted article, Loeser argues that the government needs new ways of stopping such domestic terrorist attacks, including using internet advocacy and a general reform of the legal system.

On March 9, 2010, a police officer in Greensboro, North Carolina, pulled over Tornello Fontaine Pierce El-Bey to issue a routine citation for his expired vehicle registration.[1] The officer detained Mr. Pierce during the traffic stop, cited him for the expired registration and for operating a vehicle without a license,

"From Paper Terrorists to Cop Killers: The Sovereign Citizen Threat," Charles Loeser, Reprinted with permission of North Carolina Law Review Association, Vol. 93 2015.

and released him.[2] Mr. Pierce then sued the Greensboro Police Department in federal court, alleging that the traffic stop was a violation of both the United Nations Declaration on the Rights of Indigenous Peoples[3] and the 1790 Sundry Free Moors Act,[4] and that the stop forced Pierce into "Illegal Slavery Trade (Chattel) by selling and trading Indigenous people for profit without Noble Plaintiff(s) receiving any benefit," among numerous other claims for relief.[5] This was a case of an unlucky police officer and a particularly litigious driver. Pierce's propensity for filing frivolous lawsuits has earned him notoriety in federal court—in this lawsuit, for instance, the judge derisively referred to him as a "frequent and enthusiastic litigator."[6]

[…]

In Chicago, Illinois, Cherron Phillips—who prefers to be known as River Tali El Bey—filed multiple "false maritime liens" against public officials involved in her brother's drug conspiracy case, some in amounts as high as $100 billion.[10] As Ms. Tali filed "unintelligible motions," the federal district judge told Ms. Tali that he "hesitate[d] to rank [her] statements in order of just how bizarre they are."[11] Ms. Tali has been charged with targeting U.S. Attorney Patrick Fitzgerald and several federal judges by filing false, multi-billion dollar liens on their homes.[12]

In another, less formal approach, a Las Vegas couple armed themselves with guns and secured a vacant house, planning to follow police officers and kidnap them during the course of routine traffic stops.[13] The couple planned to hold trials for the officers for civil rights violations.[14] The couple's plans were thwarted by an undercover police officer who learned of the plans and arrested them.[15]

What ties this bizarre medley of individuals together is their status as sovereign citizens. "Sovereign citizen" is a catchall identifier that refers to a wide range of anti-government individuals who share some common beliefs.[16] The sovereign citizen movement can be traced back to far-right groups like the Posse Comitatus, tax protestors, and the militia movement of the 1980s and 90s.[17] Some members' affiliation is limited to making vocal critiques of the legitimacy of federal, state, and local governments and manufacturing odd driver's licenses, license plates, and registrations.[18] Others engage in "paper terrorism"[19] and even physical violence toward government officials.[20] As the threat of sovereign citizens has grown,[21] state and local governments as well as judges have responded by imposing harsh penalties for filing false liens and imprisoning frivolous litigants for contempt of court.[22] These responses have had limited success at deterring sovereign citizens and might only be effective inasmuch as they incapacitate individual sovereign citizens for the time that the citizens are incarcerated.[23]

Because paper terrorism is so pervasive, and because it has garnered significant publicity,[24] states have begun enacting harsher penalties for filing false liens and lawsuits.[25] However, there is little evidence that these laws work to deter the subject of the sanction in particular or sovereign citizens in general.[26] The systems that are currently in place to combat sovereign citizens, namely felony lien laws, are not sufficient to control or eliminate the sovereign movement. This Comment argues that it is therefore important to explore other methods of preventing sovereign citizens from continuing to wreak havoc on the justice system. In addition to already-existing felony lien laws, governments can best counter sovereign citizens with a combination of pre-filing injunctions— what this Comment refers to as a "hard" solution—and Internet advocacy, procedural justice, and general systemic reform—what this Comment calls "soft" solutions.

[…]

From the Posse to Ruby Ridge–The Beginnings of a Far-Right Movement

Sovereign citizens ("sovereigns") can be traced back to a number of radical rightist groups, namely the Posse Comitatus, tax protestors, and more generally, the modern militia movement. These groups share fervent anti-government sentiments, often racist beliefs, and tactics such as abusing the court system to harass public officials. The similarities between contemporary sovereign citizens and the Posse Comitatus, tax protestors, or militias often render them indistinguishable at first glance; however, upon closer inspection it becomes clear that sovereign citizens arose out of these three distinct groups. It is instructive to lay out the precursors to the sovereign citizen movement for a more coherent view of how sovereign citizens act and what they believe.

The Posse Comitatus

The Posse is an important precursor to sovereign citizens, providing many foundational tactics and beliefs. Posse groups originally formed in the American Midwest to defend the Constitution by forming "common-law" courts and imprisoning public officials who purportedly acted in dereliction of the Constitution.[27] Much like Christian Identity, the white supremacist group with which the Posse shared many members,[28] the Posse Comitatus was, at its core, a "racist, anti-Semitic, antitax group that believe[d] there [was] no legitimate form of government beyond the county level."[29]

Though the Posse Comitatus began in 1969, it reached its height during the farm crisis in the 1980s by teaching legal theories and strategies to struggling farmers.[30] These strategies included suing lenders and the Federal Reserve, as well as what is now known as "paper terrorism": filing false liens against bankers, IRS agents, police officers, and other public officials.[31] Public officials can easily become targets of paper terrorism when they are engaged in any form of proceeding involving a Posse member or sovereign citizen, "from pet licensing to serious criminal charges."[32] Posse Comitatus members also practice a form of "severation," an attempt to reclaim sovereignty or "true freedom" by returning or destroying driver's licenses and other government-issued documents that allegedly "intrude upon their God-given individual rights."[33] The Posse movement largely disappeared in 1983 when a member killed two U.S. Marshals, thus placing the group under increased scrutiny by authorities.[34] However, by that time, the Posse's strategies and beliefs had taken hold and carried over to the burgeoning militia movement and, eventually, to sovereign citizens.[35]

Tax Protestors

The tax protestor movement laid important anti-government ideological foundations for sovereign citizens.[36] Tax protestors are a group of anti-government individuals who believe the income tax is illegitimate.[37] Unlike the Posse Comitatus, the tax protestor movement has "no common theological, philosophical, or racial beliefs"; rather, they subscribe to anti-tax theories that are promulgated through books, manuals, and, more recently, the Internet by for-profit theorists.[38] They argue that the income tax violates the Fifth Amendment, that the Sixteenth Amendment was never properly ratified, or that income tax applies only to residents of Washington, D.C.[39] Some individuals employ tax protestor tactics, namely litigating using these anti-tax theories, because they cannot afford to pay income tax; others seem to harbor fervent anti-government sentiments and are, more than anything, "looking for trouble with the IRS" or seeking an outlet to challenge the purportedly illegitimate federal government.[40] Also unlike the Posse, tax protestors still seem to be active and remain "thorns in the side of the federal judiciary."[41]

The Militia Movement

Examining the militia movement's origins, strategies, and downfall is helpful to understand the meteoric rise in sovereign citizens and the attention they have garnered across the country.[42] The American Militia Movement is founded on the principle that, at varying levels, the U.S. government has been corrupted—generally by the "New World Order,"[43] which secretly controls the federal government—and the revolutionary militiamen are the only capable saviors of true American values.[44] In addition to the militias' central element of conspiracism,[45] militias were, at their zenith, bound together by common membership in the Christian Identity movement.[46] Despite this common membership, not all militias held the same racist beliefs as members of Christian Identity; indeed, some militias in the early 1990s eschewed explicit racism.[47] However, by 1994, it became clear that the "links between the [militia] movement as a whole and the haters and racists of America were strong," despite the efforts of the more tolerant militias.[48]

In addition to objecting to the purported takeover of the U.S. government by agents of the New World Order or the installation of a shadow government broadly, most modern militias believe that the corrupted government has expanded impermissibly. Particularly, militia members tend to object to the Fourteenth Amendment, income tax, and any gun control legislation.[49] Militias are driven by the belief that it is their job to return U.S. government to what they believe are the ideals of its founders. They believe that resistance, including by violent means, is right and righteous.[50]

It was in this context of perceived government overreaching that federal agents seized Ruby Ridge in a deadly shootout with American citizens. This confrontation, by most accounts, led to the rise of the modern militia movement.[51] Ruby Ridge began when Randy Weaver, a survivalist who subscribed to many core militia ideologies, failed to appear in court on felony weapons charges, instigating a large-scale standoff with multiple federal agencies and local authorities.[52] Early in the standoff, agents hiding at the bottom of the Weavers' property were compromised when Weaver, Weaver's son, and Weaver's friend walked toward the hidden agents with their dog.[53] In an attempt to elude the suspects, an agent shot and killed the dog, who seemed to have picked up the agents' scent.[54] Hearing the shot, Weaver retreated, and his friend opened fire on the agents, who returned fire, killing the friend and, tragically, Weaver's fleeing son.[55] The next day, an FBI sniper saw Randy Weaver and fired at him.[56] The first shot hit Weaver in the arm, while the second shot missed Weaver and instead struck his wife, killing her.[57] After ten days and extensive negotiations, Weaver eventually surrendered to federal agents.[58] Between the deaths of Weaver's wife and son, the perception that federal agents killed

Weaver's wife and son intentionally, and the intricate conspiracy theory subsequently put forward at Weaver's trial, Ruby Ridge became the *force majeure* that vindicated militias nationwide.[59]

Sensing the potential for widespread success, a leader of the Christian Identity movement called a meeting of militia leaders across the nation in 1992 that would later be termed the "Estes Park meeting."[60] The meeting drew members of the Ku Klux Klan, Gun Owners of America, and significantly, Louis Beam, a national leader in the militia movement.[61] Though the meeting was initially pitched as a response to the perceived atrocities at Ruby Ridge, it ended up serving as a strategy session among national militia leaders.[62] The leaders narrowed the attendees' focus to ensure that the "public face of the movement . . . would focus on the victimization of innocent citizens by an abusive government," while the true motivational impetus for the members remained their "profound hatred of the national government."[63]

Militias toned down the racist and violent rhetoric that previously characterized their public image in exchange for a message that would garner increased popular support.[64] Thus, as a consequence of Ruby Ridge and the Estes Park meeting, hundreds of thousands of Americans began to openly support— or join—the militia movement without feeling like radicals or racists.[65] Equally important, leaders at the meeting—particularly Beam—proposed the formation of small, armed militias that would directly resist the government, instead of employing traditional forms of lobbying and political dissent.[66] These militias would adopt the model of "leaderless resistance," and in so doing ensure that even if the government infiltrated or disbanded one militia, members would not be able to turn over members of other militias to the authorities.[67]

Just a few months after Ruby Ridge, the federal government's large-scale, surprise raid of David Koresh's[68] Branch Davidian compound in Waco, Texas, further vindicated the militia movement.[69] After committing a series of egregious mistakes that significantly compromised the government's secret plans,[70] instead of waiting or modifying their strategy, federal agents went forward with their plan to perform a surprise raid.[71] Going forward with a "secret" raid of which the suspects were aware was predictably unsuccessful—four federal agents and six Branch Davidians were killed, and an additional twenty agents and four Davidians were injured.[72] The agents retreated after this bloodshed, and the standoff that ensued lasted an unprecedented fifty-one days and culminated in a reckless FBI strategy where agents used tanks to insert flammable tear gas into the compound, causing a massive fire.[73] The exact fatality count is unknown because no one knows exactly how many Branch Davidians were in the compound at the time of the fire, but it is undisputed that at least seventy-five men, women, and children perished in the fire.[74] Militia members and sympathizers considered the raid at Waco to be "evidence of an ongoing pattern of federal abuse and murder," and the unusually ample evidence of a cover-up "made the government guilty and the militia necessary."[75] The federal government subsequently attempted to expand gun control, which further energized the already hyperactive militias and increased extreme anti-government sentiments.[76]

The post-Waco surge of militia action culminated when Timothy McVeigh, an ardent militia supporter, bombed the Murrah Building in Oklahoma City.[77] While Ruby Ridge and Waco were more clearly assaults by the federal government that resulted in defensive militia action, the Oklahoma City bombing was essentially an offensive move. However, as with Ruby Ridge and Waco, militia members and supporters immediately began promulgating conspiracy theories that implicated the federal government.[78] Whether the bombing of the Murrah Building proved too violent for militia members' and supporters' sensibilities, or the government was not so clearly culpable, or because of some other combination of factors, the militia movement ultimately lost momentum and support by the end of the 1990s.[79]

Though the era of the violent militia was over, rightist, conspiracist, anti-government groups did not disappear; rather, they chose to change tactics from outright violence and arming for a violent government takeover to more subtle, if equally damaging, strategies. Groups calling themselves "freemen" or "common-law activists" began targeting federal, state, and local officials.[80] These tactics did occasionally include shooting at law enforcement officials but more often centered on filing false liens against public officials.[81] When county clerks would not allow false liens to be filed, militia members—or, perhaps more accurately, "freemen"— would threaten violence against the clerks and their families, or shoot their cars and slash their tires.[82] These tactics remain a large part of contemporary sovereign citizens'—descendants of the militia movement—strategies to fight what they perceive as a corrupt and overreaching government.

Sovereign Citizens

Sovereign citizens emerged after the decline of the militia movement in the late 1990s, and today the movement has some 300,000 active members, with many more who arguably fit the broadest definition of "sovereign citizen."[83] It is particularly difficult to calculate sovereign citizens' numbers, because though there are some local, organized groups of sovereign citizens,[84] the majority of sovereign citizens have no official affiliation and learn tactics through the Internet or in-person seminars.[85] In addition, because most sovereign citizens' appearances in court are pursuant to minor claims such as child support or traffic violations, it is likely that for every sovereign citizen that is apprehended or haled into court, there are many more who have not been caught breaking the law or who have been released without being recorded as such by law enforcement or the courts.[86] Indeed, many false liens are filed in rural counties where they go unnoticed, and bogus incorporations can be filed online with little to no oversight.[87] Irrespective of current membership, experts have hypothesized that sovereign citizens have been experiencing and will continue to experience a meteoric rise in membership due to economic strife, the ease of accessing materials on the Internet, and the movement's rise in prisons.[88] Indeed, "[t]he movement has proliferated beyond its traditional antigovernment base, expanding aggressively among an unlikely mix of black separatist fringe groups, disgruntled police officers and IRS agents, con artists capitalizing on the mortgage crisis, and wholly unclassifiable figures . . . ."[89] As the movement grows and diversifies, many sovereign citizens enter into groups with other sovereigns.

[…]

Beliefs

The only ubiquitous sovereign citizen belief is that federal, state, and local governments are illegitimate—indeed, most sovereign citizens believe that these governments operate illegally.[91] Much like the militia movement, sovereign citizens have constructed several elaborate conspiracy theories that purport to explain how current governments have been corrupted and why they have no lawful power.[92] The most pervasive theories, often employed together, are the "Admiralty Law Theory" and the "Redemption Theory."[93]

Sovereign citizens believe that at some point—by some accounts in the 1800s around the time of the Civil War,[94] by others in the 1930s during the Great Depression[95]—a new governmental regime based on admiralty law replaced the "common-law legal system" they ascribe to the Founding Fathers.[96] This Admiralty Law Theory in many ways echoes the militia movement's ideas about a shadow government or the New World Order; that is, both conspiracy theories ascribe a malicious motive to the government, which they claim was corrupted after its legitimate beginnings at the hands of the Founding Fathers.[97] Sovereign citizens believe they are free under a common-law regime and "slaves" under admiralty law.[98]

Redemption Theory, which, for many, is a corollary of Admiralty Law Theory, is the claim that the "federal government has enslaved its citizens by using them as collateral against foreign debt."[99] More precisely, sovereign citizens subscribing to this canon believe the United States went bankrupt when it abandoned the gold standard for currency in 1933 and began using its citizens as collateral in trade agreements with foreign nations.[100] Under this theory, the United States Treasury sets up an account for each citizen at birth and pledges some amount of money on that account.[101] This securitization creates two separate identities—the corporate account, or the "strawman," and the "common-law," or core, identity.[102] The government then pays down its loans with the money each strawman pays in taxes.[103] Sovereigns believe that any identification bearing one's name in all capital letters represents the strawman identity.[104] This includes Social Security cards, passports, driver's licenses, and tax forms.[105] Sovereign citizens thus believe that they are not bound by or to such government-issued identification and documents, as such documents represent only their strawman identity. Sovereigns believe they must split their strawman identity from their "flesh-and-blood" identity in a process they call "redemption."[106] Many sovereign citizens also believe that, under Redemption Theory, there are methods of tapping into one's strawman government account to "make fortunes with the use of certain documents."[107] The supposed methods of tapping into one's government account—commonly called "freeing money from the strawman"[108]—are some of the most popular topics for sovereign citizen seminars and Internet forums.[109]

[…]

Tactics

Sovereign citizens' belief in their ability to avoid subjection to the federal government is core to their status as sovereign. Thus, tactics to avoid consenting to the perceived oppressive government's rule are central to sovereign tactics. Sovereigns believe that individual citizens must consent to the federal government's authority and, conversely, that not consenting precludes government officials—prosecutors, judges, and police officers—from having any authority over them.[134] Sovereigns believe that they avoid consenting to the government's jurisdiction and retain their common-law identities by creating their own driver's licenses, adding their thumbprints to documents, using colons and hyphens when writing their names, adding "Bey" or "El-Bey" to their names, and creating their own licenses plates with titles like "Republic of North Carolina," "Kingdom of Heaven," and "Washitaw Nation."[135] To avoid "consenting" when forced to sign an official document, sovereign citizens will write their names, followed by "UCC 1-207" or "UCC 1-308," references to the Uniform Commercial Code, which they believe has supplanted all other constitutional and statutory law.[136] These tactics, they believe, demonstrate their status as a "flesh-and-blood" person, as opposed to the strawman personalities that official documents purportedly represent.[137] There are do-it-yourself tutorials and document templates online,[138] as well as for-profit websites to which one can send photos and, for a small fee, receive sovereign citizen identification such as birth certificates, "Motorized Conveyance Registrations," and passports.[139] These tactics could be referred to collectively as preparatory—their primary purpose appears to be to prepare sovereign citizens for interactions with public officials in order that the sovereigns not waive their sovereignty and avoid incarceration or further oppression by government agents.

When the bogus documentation fails to stop the police from pursuing charges, sovereign citizens turn to response tactics. Sovereigns will go to court, almost exclusively *pro se*, file "long and rambling,"[140] "unintelligible"[141] motions and pleadings, and generally act obstinate during their court appearances.[142] Sovereigns also almost universally reject representation by licensed lawyers, preferring instead to rely on their interpretations of select cases and Black's Law Dictionary.[143] Predictably, this behavior is often unsuccessful for the combative litigants, and thus they employ the most famous and insidious sovereign citizen tactic: paper terrorism.

Paper terrorism, the filing of fraudulent liens and frivolous lawsuits against public officials, is sovereign citizens' "weapon of choice,"[144] borrowed from their predecessors—the Posse Comitatus, militias, and freemen.[145] Anyone can file a lien under the Uniform Commercial Code, and sovereign citizens tend to file liens against the homes and land of public officials who participated in or were complicit in their legal proceedings.[146] The monetary amount of these liens tends to have no basis in reality and instead is usually in preposterous amounts like $5.1 million[147] or $100 billion.[148] Some sovereigns file false liens as a method of intimidating public officials to keep them from bothering sovereigns in the future; others seem to file liens out of spite or anger when their legal strategies do not work, evidencing a "desire to punish anyone who cross[es] them."[149]

Sovereign citizens do not cease their tactics once they have failed with police and court officials, even if the sovereigns are imprisoned for their bizarre actions or paper terrorism. The sovereign citizen movement is "thriving" in prisons, where sovereign ideologues are "successfully indoctrinat[ing] fellow prisoners."[150] Consequently, "traditional" criminals are adopting sovereign citizen tactics to try to get out of prison or to retaliate against the public officials who put them in prison.[151] Aside from incarcerated sovereign citizen proselytizers, some sovereign citizen organizations sell literature to inmates. For example, *America's Bulletin*, a sovereign citizen newsletter, sells *The Prison Packet*, a green, spiral-bound notebook filled with variations on typical sovereign citizen theories, for twenty-two dollars.[152] Chief among these theories is that "By filing a blizzard of liens and complaints . . . inmates can not only free themselves, but also walk away with hundreds of thousands of dollars."[153] In addition to the pervasive *Prison Packet*, non-inmate sovereign citizens manage to meet and proselytize to prisoners under the guise of religious outreach.[154]

Like their immediate predecessor, the militia movement, sovereign citizens have at times resorted to extreme violence, albeit much less frequently than the militia movement did. One notable recent instance of sovereign citizen violence is the case of Jerry Kane. Jerry Kane was driving through Arkansas with his son in 2010 when two police officers pulled them over.[155] After a brief argument with the officers, Kane's son exited the vehicle with an AK-47 assault rifle, then shot and killed both officers.[156] Roughly an hour and a half later the police located the Kanes, still driving their car, and engaged in a shootout, ultimately killing the Kanes.[157] What is notable about these events is that the Kanes were ostensibly average, if quite active, sovereign citizens: at the time of the shooting, the Kanes had been driving across the country giving seminars to fellow sovereign citizens on how to avoid paying taxes and how to avoid mortgage foreclosure.[158] There were no prior indications of the Kanes' violent tendencies, and it is not clear that the Kanes would have ever resorted to violence had they not been pulled over.[159] In point of fact, around the time of his death, Kane's common-law wife was involved in a (non-violent) dog-licensing dispute with the state wherein she filed ten nonsensical documents in two months.[160] Her actions resulted in the prosecutor dropping the case, which Kane's wife characterized as a victory.[161] Whether the Kanes would have continued driving around conducting trainings—or fighting municipal dog ordinances for that matter— without violence remains unclear. What is clear is the volatility of at least some seemingly ordinary sovereign citizens.

Though the Kanes may have thrust sovereign citizens back into the focus of law enforcement and the public, their case was certainly not the first instance of sudden and extreme sovereign citizen violence. In 1995, a sovereign citizen in Ohio pulled a gun on a police officer, who then killed the citizen.[162] Two years later, a New Hampshire sovereign citizen killed two police officers and two civilians, and wounded three additional officers before killing himself.[163] In 1999, a sovereign citizen in Alabama shot and killed a police officer who encountered him sleeping in a parked car.[164] Most recently, in August of 2013, a Las Vegas sovereign citizen couple conspired to kidnap police officers and detain them in a makeshift jail they had constructed in their home.[165] Though these incidents of violence are relatively sporadic, particularly considering the strength of the sovereign citizen movement, they tend to show that affiliation with a far-right anti-government group can prove to be highly volatile at a moment's notice.

Stopping the Sovereign Citizen Threat

As the sovereign citizen movement grows, bringing with it increased violence and paper terrorism, law enforcement and court officials have scrambled to find effective methods to deter and punish sovereign citizens. Some notable methods include the increase in the grade of crime—misdemeanor to felony—or punishment for filing fraudulent or frivolous liens, and the move to allow clerks discretion in deciding whether to accept liens.[166] Though this type of law fulfills the retributivist goal of punishing offenders for their crimes,[167] the deterrent effect is questionable. That is, how effectively can a law deter offenders who do not believe in the validity of the government or its laws? This Comment argues for the necessity of "soft" solutions—in addition to heightened punishment—to curb sovereign citizens' litigiousness, not only because of the probable ineffectiveness of deterrence, but also because even incarceration is probably counterproductive because of the prevalence of sovereign citizen proselytization in prisons.[168]

[…]

Soft Solutions

The sovereign citizen movement shows no signs of letting up in recruitment, paper terrorism, or violent tactics. In addition to increasing punishments for filing fraudulent liens—the net effect of which remains to be seen—and judiciously using gatekeeper orders, there are a number of "soft" solutions that could prove useful against this resilient threat. This subsection starts by addressing procedural justice as one "soft" solution, and then proceeds in Subpart 2 to discuss the possibilities of general systemic reform.

[…]

General Systemic Reform

Inasmuch as individuals are vulnerable to indoctrination by sovereign citizen ideologies because of poor economic conditions,[215] it is important to ensure there are governmental support systems in place, particularly when there is economic downturn. Having government-sponsored safety nets can prevent unfortunate circumstances, like home foreclosures, that often drive people to sovereign citizen circles in search of solutions.[216] In addition, ensuring that primary and secondary schools teach effective and extensive history and political science may prevent certain people from being susceptible to sovereign citizen ideologies. For instance, more effectively teaching students about the basic nature and structure of government might prevent them from later thinking that they are not bound by the Constitution if they do not sign it.[217] There are certainly sovereign citizens whose blog and video postings on the Internet suggest familiarity with such topics as political science and history,[218] though they presumably learned much of what they believe after and outside of the confines of early education. It is similarly possible that some sovereign citizens learned basic civics and social studies in school and then later rejected it as false or unreliable.

More concretely, given the importance of the Internet for sovereign citizen recruitment and training,[219] it follows that the Internet might also be a locus of prevention. To prevent ordinary citizens from becoming ensnared in a web of sovereign citizen propaganda, some strategists have suggested basic online activism.[220] That is, it is problematic that "someone searching the Internet for 'UCC sovereign taxes' or 'redemption debtor' is led to a rat's nest of antigovernment extremist sites" with very few factually based articles to dissuade the searcher.[221] Providing increased access to reputable information about the harms of sovereign citizen ideologies and tactics could instead lead to prospective sovereign citizens finding articles that "scream 'scam' and 'fraud,' " like the results one encounters when searching something like "Nigerian investment E-mail."[222] Though sovereign citizens have a hyperactive Internet presence—including seething responses to critical articles from websites like that of the Southern Poverty Law Center[223]—a proliferation of more elucidative articles would at least signal to unsure parties that there is cause to be wary.

It may seem intellectually lazy or overly idealistic to suggest somewhat nebulous, large-scale systemic fixes for the problem of sovereign citizens. However, deterrence is particularly difficult for sovereign citizens, and incarceration may be counterproductive.[224] Systemic reforms, along with other soft solutions and gatekeeper orders, are important steps to take in preventing the continued growth of the sovereign citizen movement.

Conclusion

Sovereign citizens are the latest development in a genealogy of anti-government, largely racist, conspiracy theorists that cause public officials significant problems. At their most harmless, they frustrate police officers with phony identification cards and insist that they are not corporations.[225] At their most harmful, they lure police officers into traps and murder them for the alleged injustices law enforcement has perpetrated against sovereigns. And most commonly, sovereign citizens hold up court proceedings with incomprehensible jargon and theories and sue public officials when their cases get dismissed.

States' responses to sovereign citizens have been dominated by stringent laws that punish the filing of frivolous liens and lawsuits. To be sure, there is value in deterring paper terrorism and punishing those who engage in it. However, there is little indication that these laws have any deterrent effect, and it is therefore crucial that state legislatures and state and federal courts consider other tactics to quell the sovereign citizen movement. Pre-filing injunctions provide a concrete fix for repeat litigants, who congest courts with their abusive and frivolous filings. These, in addition to various soft solutions like procedural justice, general systemic reform, and Internet activism, have a strong chance of being more effective than felony lien laws alone. Sovereign citizens may go extinct on their own like the militia movement, but while they exist it is crucial to control their terroristic tendencies to save public officials' money, time, and, in extreme cases, lives.

References

[1]. El-Bey v. City of Greensboro, No. 1:10CV291, 2010 WL 3242193, at *1 (M.D.N.C. Aug. 16, 2010), *report and recommendation adopted as modified*, No. 1:10CV291, 2011 WL 255719 (M.D.N.C. Jan. 25, 2011). "El-Bey" is a suffix that many sovereign citizens adopt. *See infra* Part II.B. For the sake of clarity, this Comment will refer to the litigant by his legally-recognized surname, Pierce. *El-Bey*, 2010 WL 3242193, at *1. Like many of the sovereign citizens' practices, adding "El-Bey" to one's name has a different meaning and rationale depending upon whom one asks. *See, e.g.*, A. Melek Özyetgin, *On the Use of the Title "Beg" Among the Turks*, 11 Int'l J. Cent. Asian Stud. 156, 158 n.4, 159 n.8 (2006) ("In the Old Turkic period, *beg*, was the title of people who headed small tribes or large communities comprising various tribes . . . . Today the word represents respect when used as *bey* after male names and as a form of address . . . ."); R.V. Bey, *What to Study, Moors in America*, R.V. Bey Publications, http://rvbeypublications.com/id80.html (last updated Jan. 10, 2015, 2:12 AM) ("Moors are the Title holders. The Titles are El, Bey, Dey, Al, and Ali. Translated as the 5 civilized so-called Indian tribes during the battles on the Western Frontier, here in North America.").

[2]. *El-Bey*, 2010 WL 3242193, at *1.

[3]. G.A. Res. 61/295, Annex, U.N. GAOR, 61st Sess., Supp. No. 49 (Vol. III), U.N. Doc. A/61/49 (Vol. III), at 16 (Sept. 13, 2007).

[4]. The complaint's reference to the fictitious "*1790 Sundry Free Moors Act*," Complaint at 4, *El-Bey*, 2010 WL 3242193 (No. 1:10CV291), *available at* http://www.digtriad.com/news/pdf/ticket-lawsuit.pdf, is particularly intriguing. While, to the best of this author's knowledge, no such legislation was ever enacted, archive records from the South Carolina General Assembly's House Journals do mention a bizarre incident in 1790:

petition was presented to the House [of Representatives] from Sundry Free Moors, Subjects of the Emperor of Morocco; and residents in this State, praying that in case they should Commit Any Fault amenable to be brought to Justice, that they as Subjects to a Prince in Alliance with the United States of America, may be tried under the same Laws as the Citizens of this State would be liable to be tried, and not under the Negro Act.

Journal, 8th Gen. Assemb., 2d Sess. 363 (S.C. 1790). This so called "petition of the Free Moors" was referred to a committee of several House members, including the well-known General Charles Pinckney, which in turn [r]eport[ed] that they have Considered the same and are of opinion that no Law of this State can in its Construction or Operation apply to [the Free Moors], and that persons who were Subjects of the Emperor of Morocco being Free in this State are not triable by the Law for the better Ordering and Governing of Negroes and other Slaves.

Id. at 373–74. It appears that the committee's findings were well received, as the Journal indicates it was thereafter "Resolved That this House do agree with the Report." *Id.* at 374.

[5]. Complaint, *supra* note 4, at 1–4. Nearly all materials written by sovereign citizens are riddled with typographical errors. *See, e.g., id.*; Anti-Defamation League, The Lawless Ones: The Resurgence of the Sovereign Citizen Movement 7 (2d ed. 2012) (describing tactics of self-identified sovereign citizen "David Wynn Miller, who has actually created (and uses) a completely alternative grammar for the English language, which he claims allows him to master the judicial system. Or, as Miller puts it on his Web site, 'FOR THIS PLENIPOTENTIARY-JUDGE: David-Wynn: Miller's-KNOWLEDGE OF THESE CORRECT-SENTENCE-STRUCTURES-COMMUNICATION-SYNTAX-LANGUAGE=(C.-S.-S.-C.-S.-L.) IS WITH THE CLAIMS BY THE QUANTUM-LANGUAGE-SYNTAX-NOW-TIME-FACTS.' ").The quoted material in this Comment retains the original capitalization, spelling, and grammar unless otherwise noted. The notation "sic" or other alterations are reserved for instances where confusion is likely.

[10]. Annie Sweeney & Jason Meisner, *Chicago Woman's Trial Could Get Wild*, Chi. Trib. (Aug. 2, 2013), http://articles.chicagotribune.com/2013-08-02/news/ct-met-sovereign -citizen-trial-20130728_1_chicago-woman-then-chief-judge-james-holderman-court -rules.

[11]. *Id.*

[12]. *Id.*

[13]. Erin McClam, *Vegas Arrests Cast Light on Anti-Government 'Sovereign Citizens' Movement*, NBC News (Aug. 23, 2013, 10:39 AM), http://usnews.nbcnews.com/_ news/2013/08/23/20151351-vegas-arrests-cast-light-on-anti-government-sovereign -citizens-movement?lite.

[14]. *Id.*

[15]. *Id.*

[16]. *A Quick Guide to Sovereign Citizens*, UNC Sch. Gov't 1 (Sept. 2012), http://www .sog.unc.edu/sites/www.sog.unc.edu/files/R09.1%20Sovereign%20citizens%20briefing%20 paper%20Sept%2012%20%28Crowell%29.pdf [hereinafter SOG I]. For instance, sovereign citizens generally believe that the United States government is illegitimate, that they are not subject to its laws, and that they can circumvent its laws in bizarre ways, ranging from claiming immunity based on a fictitious, eighteenth-century treaty between the United States and Morocco to renouncing the legality of all government documentation in which their names are written in all capital letters. *See id.* at 1–3.

[17]. Francis X. Sullivan, Comment, *The "Usurping Octopus of Jurisdictional/Authority": The Legal Theories of the Sovereign Citizen Movement*, 1999 Wis. L. Rev. 785, 786–87; *see infra* Part I.

[18]. *See* SOG I, *supra* note 16, at 1, 3.

[19]. "Paper terrorism" refers to the filing of false liens and frivolous claims against public officials. *See, e.g.*, Erica Goode, *In Paper War, Flood of Liens Is the Weapon*, N.Y. Times (Aug. 23, 2013), http://www.nytimes.com/2013/08/24/us/citizens-without-a-country -wage-battle-with-liens.html?_r=0.

[20]. *See, e.g.*, SOG I, *supra* note 16, at 1; Counterterrorism Analysis Section, FBI, *Sovereign Citizens: A Growing Domestic Threat to Law Enforcement*, FBI L. Enforcement Bull., Sept. 2011, at 20, 20–21 [hereinafter FBI], *available at* http://leb.fbi.gov/2011/ september/leb-september-2011.

[21]. Casey Sanchez, *Sovereign Citizens Movement Resurging: Resurgence of Far-Right Movement Reported*, S. Poverty L. Center, http://www.splcenter.org/get -informed/intelligence-report/browse-all-issues/2009/spring/return-of-the-sovereigns (last visited Apr. 9, 2015) ("The movement has proliferated beyond its traditional antigovernment base, expanding aggressively among an unlikely mix of black separatist fringe groups, disgruntled police officers and IRS agents, [and] con artists capitalizing on the mortgage crisis . . . .").

[22]. *See, e.g.*, Goode, supra note 19.

[23]. *See id.* However, prison may not even incapacitate sovereign citizens, as experts have observed sovereign citizen recruitment and indoctrination in prisons. *See* SOG I, *supra* note 16, at 3; Sanchez, *supra* note 21.

[24]. *See, e.g.*, Caitlin Dickson, *Sovereign Citizens Are America's Top Cop-Killers*, Daily Beast (Nov. 25, 2014), http://www.thedailybeast.com/articles/2014/11/25/sovereign -citizens-are-america-s-top-cop-killers.html; Goode, supra note 19; McClam, *supra* note 13; Sweeney & Meisner, *supra* note 10; Sanchez, *supra* note 21.

[25]. Goode, *supra* note 19.

[26]. *See* Mark Pitcavage, *Paper Terrorism's Forgotten Victims: The Use of Bogus Liens Against Private Individuals and Businesses*, Anti-Defamation League (June 29, 1998),

http://archive.adl.org/mwd/privlien.html (last modified June 29, 1998) (exploring the efficacy of methods employed to combat the filing of false liens).

[27]. *See* Sullivan, *supra* note 17, at 787.

[28]. *Id.* Christian Identity is an anti-Semitic, racist movement that began after World War II and dissolved by the 1990s. Michael Barkun, *Essay: The Christian Identity Movement*, S. Poverty L. Center, http://www.splcenter.org/get-informed/intelligence-files/ideology/christian-identity/the-christian-identity-movement (last visited Apr. 9, 2015). Adherents promulgated theologically unique, racist beliefs, including the view that the biblical story of Adam as the progenitor of humanity only involved the creation of whites and that other races were created separately. *Id.* Moreover, members of Christian Identity believed they were in a battle against non-whites and Jews alike. *Id.* Sects of Christian Identity engaged in militaristic training, and some even attempted to instigate race wars. *Id.*

[29]. Morris Dees with James Corcoran, Gathering Storm: America's Militia Threat 14 (1996).

[30]. *See* Sullivan, *supra* note 17, at 787–88.

[31]. *Id.* at 788.

[32]. Lorelei Laird, *'Sovereign Citizens' Plaster Courts with Bogus Legal Filings—and Some Turn to Violence*, A.B.A. J. (May 1, 2014, 10:20 AM), http://www.abajournal .com/magazine/article/sovereign_citizens_plaster_courts_with_bogus_legal_filings/.

[33]. Dees with Corcoran, *supra* note 29, at 87; *see also* Keith Schneider, *Terror in Oklahoma: The Far Right; Bomb Echoes Extremists' Tactics*, N.Y. Times (Apr. 26, 1995), http://www.times.com/1995/04/26/us/terror-in-oklahoma-the-far-right-bomb-echoes -extremists-tactics.html (describing "severation" as an initiation tactic adopted by far-right extremists "who believe that only through severing all ties to [the] government can they truly be free").

[34]. *See* Sanchez, *supra* note 21; Dees with Corcoran, *supra* note 29, at 14.

[35]. Sanchez, *supra* note 21.

[36]. *See* Sullivan, *supra* note 17, at 786.

[37]. *Tax Protest Movement*, Anti-Defamation League, http://archive.adl.org/learn/ext_us/ tpm.html (last updated 2005).

[38]. Sullivan, *supra* note 17, at 789 (citing McLaughlin v. Comm'r, 832 F.2d 986, 987 (7th Cir. 1987)); *Tax Protest Movement*, *supra* note 37. There are a handful of particularly well-known tax protestors, perhaps most famous of whom is Irwin Schiff—who, despite having served time in prison, continues to hold for-profit anti-tax seminars. *Id.* Mr. Schiff is currently in federal prison for tax-related offenses. Peter J. Reilly, *Are Tax Protestors Actually Winning?*, Forbes (Jan. 17, 2013), http://www.forbes.com/sites/ peterjreilly/2013/01/17/are-tax-protesters-actually-winning/.

[39]. *Tax Protest Movement*, *supra* note 37. There are myriad arguments that claim the invalidity of income tax. One particularly interesting theory is that income tax is unconstitutional because it "place[s] the taxpayer in a position of involuntary servitude" in violation of the Thirteenth Amendment. *Id.* Another theory is that requiring individuals to fill out tax forms violates the First Amendment's free speech protections. *Id.*

[40]. *See* Sullivan, *supra* note 17, at 790 (citing Miller v. United States, 868 F.2d 236, 237–38 (7th Cir. 1989)).

[41]. McLaughlin v. Comm'r, 832 F.2d 986, 987 (7th Cir. 1987); *see also, e.g.*, Davis v. I.R.S., 905 F. Supp. 2d 1253, 1254–55 (D.N.M. 2012) (striking a plaintiff tax protestor's affidavit and dismissing the case summarily after the plaintiff "espous[ed] his alleged belief in tax-protestor rhetoric that has long been rejected in the Courts").

[42]. *See, e.g.*, Maxwell Barna, *Move Over Jihadists—Sovereign Citizens Seen as America's Top Terrorist Threat*, Vice News (Aug. 15, 2014), https://news.vice.com/article/move-over -jihadists-sovereign-citizens-seen-as-americas-top-terrorist-threat.

[43]. The "New World Order" is a popular conspiracy theory that posits that there is one unified, "shadow government" or group of actors controlling major world events and seemingly sovereign national governments. *See* Hua Hsu, *A Global Government Is Waiting in the Wings*, N.Y. Mag. (Nov. 17, 2013), http://nymag.com/news/features/conspiracy -theories/new-world-order/.

[44]. Lane Crothers, Rage on the Right: The American Militia Movement from Ruby Ridge to Homeland Security 2 (2003). The modern militia movement draws on the popular and inaccurate myth surrounding the American Revolution—that "gentle, selfless people" left their home to fight in militias, and those militias helped win the Revolution. *Id.* at 25. In reality, militias were quite ineffective in battle, and the British were defeated by "professional armies . . . and navies" with little help from militias. *Id.* at 26–27. Militia members generally believe that the "shadow government" acts at the behest of some "other," often the United Nations. *Id.* at 12. Shadow agents are believed to have infiltrated all branches of American government. *Id.* at 57.

[45]. *See id.* at 42 (explaining that militias are characterized by a "conspiracism" mindset that "elevates the scapegoat to the role of an organized plotter engaged in systemic acts of evil to deny rights and freedoms to the 'good' people in society").

[46]. *See* Dees with Corcoran, *supra* note 29, at 18. For background on the Christian Identity movement, see *supra* note 28 and accompanying text.

[47]. *See* Dees with Corcoran, *supra* note 29, at 86–87.

[48]. *Id.* at 87.

[49]. Crothers, *supra* note 44, at 51–53.

[50]. *See id.* at 2.

[51]. *Id.* at 97.

[52]. Dees with Corcoran, *supra* note 29, at 9. For more detailed accounts of Ruby Ridge, see generally id. at 9–27 and Crothers, *supra* note 44, at 75–92.

[53]. Crothers, *supra* note 44, at 82.

[54]. *Id.*

[55]. *Id.*

[56]. *Id.* at 84.

[57]. *Id.*

[58]. *Id.* at 87.

[59]. *Id.* at 90. Weaver's defense attorneys managed to exclude much of Weaver's racism and religious fanaticism from his trial, thereby portraying Weaver as an innocent citizen wronged by a violent and vengeful government. *Id.*

[60]. *Id.* at 93–94.

[61]. *Id.*; *see also* Dees with Corcoran, *supra* note 29, at 33–35 (explaining Beam's status as a national leader in the Militia Movement in addition to being the Grand Dragon of the Texas Knights of the Ku Klux Klan and its paramilitary group, the Texas Emergency Reserve).

[62]. Crothers, *supra* note 44, at 93–95.

[63]. *Id.* at 94.

[64]. *Id.*; *see* Dees with Corcoran, *supra* note 29, at 58–59.

[65]. Crothers, *supra* note 44, at 94–95.

[66]. *Id.* at 94.

[67]. *Id.*; *see also* Schneider, *supra* note 33 (" 'Leaderless resistance' refers to the need to keep the planning of terrorist attacks confined to individuals or very small groups to prevent infiltration by the police.").

[68]. David Koresh was the eventual leader of the Branch Davidians and professed to be a prophet—specifically, the Lamb referenced in the Book of Revelation. Malcolm Gladwell, *Sacred and Profane*, New Yorker (Mar. 31, 2014), http://www.newyorker .com/magazine/2014/03/31/sacred-and-profane-4. Problematically for the FBI, the Branch Davidians *believed* Koresh was the Lamb, which the FBI likened to the situation of Jim Jones' cult followers before their mass suicide. *Id.*

[69]. Dees with Corcoran, *supra* note 29, at 72; *see* Crothers, *supra* note 44, at 114.

[70]. Federal agents planned to storm the Branch Davidian compound by hiding in "cattle trucks that would pull up close to the [compound] buildings as if lost. Then, when the Branch Davidians least expected it, the agents would deploy, execute a dynamic assault on the property, and arrest Koresh." Crothers, *supra* note 44, at 104. However, the agents committed a laundry list of blunders that completely eliminated the element of surprise: the hotels in Waco "filled with heavily armed ATF agents" days before the raid; a reporter asked a mailman for directions to the compound, explaining that a raid was being launched later that day, causing the mailman, a Branch Davidian, to go warn other members; and a helicopter began circling the compound early in the morning in anticipation of the raid. *Id.*at 105.

[71]. *Id.* at 104–05.

[72]. *Id.* at 105–06.

[73]. *Id.* at 109–10. For a more detailed account of the standoff and final raid, see id. at 104–110.

[74]. *Id.* at 110.

[75]. Dees with Corcoran, *supra* note 29, at 73; Crothers, *supra* note 44, at 116. For a list of the ostensible evidence of a cover-up, see Crothers, *supra* note 44, at 116–18.

[76]. *See* Crothers, supra note 44, at 121–22 (listing significant actions militias took nationwide in response to Waco).

[77]. *Id.* at 123–26. It is important to note that the Oklahoma City bombing is not merely correlated with Ruby Ridge and Waco because it was a successive event inspired by anti-government animus; McVeigh expressly admitted to being strongly influenced by the events at Ruby Ridge and Waco to mastermind and perpetrate the attack. *Id.* at 128–29.

[78]. *Id.* at 134–35. These conspiracy theories included ideas of a general cover-up, like with Waco, as well as theories that the United Nations was involved or that the government bombed the Murrah Building to frame the militia movement. *Id.* Others, like Louis Beam, blamed the government in more indirect ways:

Blaming the bombing in Oklahoma City on the militia, or unnamed 'patriots,' is an obscenity . . . [f]or it was, after all, the taking of lives by the government at Ruby Ridge and Waco that provided the innocent blood that gave birth to the militia and the associated anti-government feeling currently sweeping the nation.

Dees with Corcoran, *supra* note 29, at 174.

[79]. Crothers, supra note 44, at 141.

[80]. *Id.* at 142–43.

[81]. *Id.*; *see* James Brooke, *Officials Say Montana 'Freemen' Collected $1.8 Million in Scheme*, N.Y. Times (Mar. 29, 1996), http://www.nytimes.com/1996/03/29/us/officials-say -montana-freemen-collected-1.8-million-in-scheme.html?src=pm.

[82]. Crothers, *supra* note 44, at 142–43.

[83]. *See Sovereign Citizens Movement*, S. Poverty L. Center, http://www.splcenter.org/ get-informed/intelligence-files/ideology/sovereign-citizens-movement (last visited Apr. 9, 2015) [hereinafter SPLC I].

[84]. Several of these groups are discussed in more detail *infra* text accompanying note 90.

[85]. SPLC I, *supra* note 83.

[86]. *See, e.g., id.*; FBI, *supra* note 19, at 22; Sullivan, *supra* note 17, at 798.

[87]. Sanchez, *supra* note 21 ("Many bogus liens are filed in rural county courts, where officials with little or no knowledge of the movement often fail to notice them. Fake incorporation papers, among other legal documents, can be filed digitally with state business bureaus with virtually no oversight.").

[88]. *See* SPLC I, *supra* note 83; FBI, *supra* note 19, at 23; Sanchez, *supra* note 21; *see also*Goode, *supra* note 19 (" 'The convergence of the evidence strongly suggests a movement that is flourishing . . . . It is present in every single state in the country.' ").

[89]. Sanchez, *supra* note 21.

[91]. *See, e.g.*, Goode, *supra* note 19; FBI, *supra* note 19, at 20.

[92]. *See* SOG I, *supra* note 16, at 1–3; SPLC I, *supra* note 83.

[93]. *See* SPLC I, *supra* note 83; SOG I, *supra* note 16, at 2.

[94]. SOG I, *supra* note 16, at 2.

[95]. SPLC I, *supra* note 83.

[96]. *Id.*

[97]. *See* Hsu, *supra* note 43; text accompanying note 43.

[98]. *See* Hsu, *supra* note 43; text accompanying note 43. It is unclear why sovereign citizens believe the current legal system is one of admiralty law, or whether proponents of the theory understand what admiralty law is; similarly, it is not clear what makes the system sovereigns believe in a "common-law" system. Irrespective of their understanding, vocal sovereign citizens consistently reference illegitimate "admiralty" or "maritime" law. *See* SOG I, *supra* note 16, at 4–5 (listing the words and phrases sovereign citizens commonly use in court filings and documents, such as "In Admiralty" and "Notice of International Commerce Claim Within The Admiralty . . .").

[99]. Sanchez, *supra* note 21.

[100]. FBI, *supra* note 19, at 21.

[101]. SOG I, *supra* note 16, at 2.

[102]. *Id.*

[103]. *Id.*

[104]. *Id.* [105]. *Id.*

[106]. SPLC I, *supra* note 83. The process of "redemption" is discussed *infra* Part II.A.

[107]. Sanchez, *supra* note 21; J.J. MacNab, *'Sovereign' Citizen Kane*, S. Poverty L. Center (2010), http://www.splcenter.org/get-informed/intelligence-report/browse-all-issues/2010/ fall/sovereign-citizen-kane [hereinafter SPLC II], ("[B]y filing a series of complex, legal-sounding documents, the sovereign [believes he] can tap into that secret Treasury account for his own purposes. Over the last 30 years, there have been hundreds of sovereign promoters packaging different combinations of forms and paperwork, attempting to perfect the process.").

[108]. FBI, *supra* note 19, at 21–22.

[109]. *See id.*

134]. *See* SOG I, *supra* note 16, at 2.

[135]. *See id.* at 3–4; Goode, *supra* note 19.

[136]. *See* Sanchez, *supra* note 21; *see also* SOG I, *supra* note 16, at 5 (listing UCC 1-207 as a sovereign citizen "buzzword").

[137]. SPLC I, *supra* note 83.

[138]. *See, e.g.,* Freedom Documents, http://keystoliberty2.wordpress.com/ (last visited Apr. 9, 2015) (providing templates for documents to submit to the IRS and other government agencies in order to retain sovereign status).

[139]. *See, e.g.,* SPLC III, *supra* note 133 (describing the Washitaw Nation's lucrative false document production business).

[140]. Procup v. Strickland, 792 F.2d 1069, 1070 (11th Cir. 1986).

[141]. Goode, *supra* note 19.

[142]. *See, e.g.,* Sweeney & Meisner, *supra* note 10 ("Judge Shadur, sitting at a conference table in his courtroom in shirtsleeves, explained in excruciating detail to Phillips the process of picking a jury and general trial procedures. 'I do not consent to the procedure,' Phillips said in a matter-of-fact tone."); Complaint at 3–4, Pierce El-Bey v. City of Greensboro, No. 1:10CV291 (M.D.N.C. Apr. 16, 2010), *available at* http://www.digtriad.com/news/pdf/ticket-lawsuit.pdf (listing the sovereign citizen Plaintiff's outlandish causes of action, including "[i]ntentional infliction of Emotional Distress and deliberately inflicted emotional distress on Plaintiff by interfering with his rights and conspiring against him, thereby destroying his trust in the judicial system"); Sanchez, *supra* note 21 ("Even as he faced the possibility of serious prison time, [sovereign citizen] Gonzalez didn't hold back, ripping up a copy of the Bill of Rights on the witness stand and sarcastically telling the judge: 'You want me to say I learned my lesson? I did. The lesson is you don't fuck with the government.' ").

[143]. *See Do You Need a Lawyer?*, Natural-Person, http://www.natural-person.ca/lawyer.html (last visited Apr. 6, 2015) ("If you use a Lawyer, you remain within the artificial-person domain and therefore are subject to the full force of all the statute laws. You only have a small chance of winning any proceedings, and usually at great expense, because you have to deal with every law, most of which have taken away the rights and freedoms of the natural-person."); *see also* SOG I, *supra* note 16, at 2 ("A sovereign citizen may carry a copy of Black's Law Dictionary as a reference resource for their common law views."); *Proof That You Are Legally Dumb*, YouTube (Dec. 24, 2013), http://www.youtube.com/watch?v=PV7XvhLMvHU&feature=c4-overview&list=UUxvxkNaSYrTqRBYGq71YCOg (depicting a sovereign citizen interpreting entries from Black's Law Dictionary).

[144]. SPLC II, *supra* note 107.

[145]. *See supra* Part I.A.

[146]. Goode, *supra* note 19.

[147]. *Id.*

[148]. Sweeney & Meisner, *supra* note 10.

[149]. United States v. Ulloa, 511 F. App'x 105, 108 (2d Cir. 2013) (describing one particular sovereign citizen's vindictive motive); *see, e.g.,* Goode, *supra* note 19 (observing that liens are "being employed more frequently as a way to retaliate against perceived injustices").

[150]. Sanchez, *supra* note 21.

[151]. *Id.*

[152]. *Id.*

[153]. *Id.*

[154]. *Id.*

[155]. SPLC II, *supra* note 107.

[156]. *Id.*

[157]. *Id.*

[158]. *Id.*

[159]. *See id.* ("Kane had met a Floridian named Donna Lee Wray at one of his foreclosure seminars three months earlier, and they had fallen in love. Father and son were headed, they thought, to a bright new life.").

[160]. *Id.*

[161]. *Id.*

[162]. *Id.*

[163]. *Id.*

[164]. *Selected Incidents of Lone Wolf Violence and Terrorism in the U.S.*, Anti-Defamation League (Apr. 14, 2014), http://www.adl.org/combating-hate/domestic-extremism -terrorism/c/selected-incidents-of-lone-wolf-violence.html.

[165]. McClam, *supra* note 13.

[166]. *See, e.g.*, Goode, *supra* note 19 ("More than a dozen states have enacted laws giving state filing offices more discretion in accepting liens, and an increasing number of states have passed or are considering legislation to toughen the penalties for bogus filings."). Before these laws, secretaries of state, and thus clerks and other filing agencies, had no discretion and were forced to accept any lien without assessing its validity. *See id.*

[167]. *Cf.* Matthew Haist, *Deterrence in a Sea of "Just Deserts": Are Utilitarian Goals Achievable in a World of "Limiting Retributivism"?*, 99 J. Crim. L. & Criminology 789, 793–94 (2009) (describing the retributivist theory of criminal justice).

[168]. *See supra* Part II.B.

[215]. *Cf.* John W. Schoen, *Study: 1.2 Million Households Lost to Recession*, NBC News (Apr. 8, 2010), http://www.nbcnews.com/id/36231884/ns/business-eye_on_the_economy/ t/study-million-households-lost-recession/#.VNtfvFPF8mU (reporting no influence of sovereign citizen ideologies on foreclosure victims of the 2008 recession).

[216]. *See, e.g.*, Goode, *supra* note 19 (" 'It seemed like we were being attacked every day,' [sovereign citizen Eilertson] said. 'We needed some way to stop the foreclosure.' ").

[217]. *See, e.g.*, Stroud, *supra* note 119 ("However, people continue to argue to this day that through the constitution (which we never signed), we all consent to be governed, because we use government sidewalks, we call the police when we are injured, ect [sic] . . . however, do we really consent?").

[218]. *See, e.g.*, *14th Amendment Citizenship: Citizen = SLAVE*, YouTube (Jan. 1, 2008), http://www.youtube.com/watch?v=y4xV4MTnCdc (citing various passages of the U.S. Constitution and the Founders' intent in an attempt to bolster sovereign citizen claims).

[219]. *See supra* notes 83–85 and accompanying text.

[220]. *See, e.g.*, Sanchez, *supra* note 21.

[221]. *Id.*

[222]. *Id.*

[223]. *See, e.g.*, A Response to Southern Poverty Law Center's Finch and Flowers 'OPINION' Regarding Sovereignty, R.V. Bey Publications, http://www.rvbeypublications. com/sitebuildercontent/sitebuilderfiles/aresponsetofinchflowers.pub.pdf (last visited Mar. 16, 2015) ("This is the third report we have seen over the past 3 years from the Southern Poverty Law Center. We urge you all to keep in mind that these are their opinions and are not in fact Law!").

[224]. *See supra* Parts II.B, III.A.

[225]. *See, e.g.*, SOG I, *supra* note 16, at 2 ("A sovereign citizen named Fred Jones may say 'I am agent of Fred Jones' to inform you that he is not the corporate entity strawman FRED JONES and thus is beyond the court's jurisdiction.").

9

Lone Wolf Attackers Are On the Rise

The Southern Poverty Law Center (SPLC)

Founded by civil rights lawyers Morris Dees and Joseph Levin Jr. in 1971, the Southern Poverty Law Center (SPLC) has won numerous landmark victories for "the exploited, the powerless and the forgotten."

In this excerpt from a special report called "Age of the Wolf," compiled by the Southern Poverty Law Center, the rising phenomenon of the lone wolf attacker is explored. According to this report, lone wolf attackers have been on the rise since the 1980s and, worrisomely, are more likely to conduct attacks based both on Islamic fundamentalism and radical conservative or Christian beliefs. As part of a study conducted by the SPLC, domestic terrorism is occurring more frequently now than in past years, largely because lone wolf attacks are more difficult to prevent than attacks planned by groups of people.

At 2:22 a.m. on the morning after Thanksgiving, a man named Larry Steve McQuilliams, clad in a tactical vest and backpack hydration unit and armed with a semi-automatic AK-47, opened fire in Austin, Texas. He unleashed more than 100 rounds, first at a federal courthouse, then at the local Mexican consulate that he also tried to firebomb, and finally at the Austin Police Department headquarters.

Before he could harm anyone, the 49-year-old McQuilliams was killed by a near-miraculous pistol shot fired by an officer standing

312 feet away. When police searched his body and his van, they found another long gun, hundreds of rounds of ammunition, a map of 34 downtown buildings that appeared to be his targets and a book and note indicating he saw himself as a "Phineas priest," a white supremacist who believes he's been personally called on by God to kill his enemies.

On his chest were the black-inked words, "Let Me Die."

McQuilliams' note said little more than that he was acting as a "priest in the fight against anti-God people." Because he had apparently spoken to no one about his plans and had no help, it's unlikely that much more about him will be learned—beyond the fact that he was a "lone wolf," the very hardest kind of terrorist to stop.

"What keeps me up at night," said Austin Police Chief Art Acevedo, who called McQuilliams an "American extremist," "is these guys. The lone wolf."

The lone wolf. Going back at least to the 1980s, that concept—a person who carries out a terrorist attack entirely on his own—has taken root on the American non-Islamic radical right and even among many jihadists. In an age of instant communications and ever more tightly knit societies, the lone wolf style of attack is vastly more likely to be successful than the kind that was once literally planned in rooms full of men, sometimes by major group leaders. People who join criminal conspiracies today are more likely than ever to be caught. As a result, there has been a long-running trend toward the lone wolf and away from group action.

A major Southern Poverty Law Center (SPLC) study of domestic terrorism over the last six years confirms this trend in dramatic fashion. Surveying 63 incidents culled from academic databases and the SPLC's own files, 46 of them—fully 74%—were carried out by lone wolves, unassisted by others. And only one of the remaining 16 (in one case, the number of attackers is not known) was planned by a named organization. In most of those 16 cases, terrorists worked in pairs—a couple, a pair of friends, two brothers and a father and son, among them—with only six involving three or more. That means that 90% percent of the 62 cases where the number of perpetrators is known were the work of one or two people.

The Study

Analyzing terrorism comes fraught with pitfalls. There is no hard and fast agreement on what constitutes a terrorist action. What if the attack has a political dimension, but is carried out by someone who is clearly mentally ill? Is a rampage killing spree terrorism or simply an eruption of personal hatreds? Does the murder of three police officers responding to a domestic disturbance count, even if the killer does have a long history in the police-hating antigovernment movement?

To get a sense of the shape of contemporary domestic terrorism—both from the radical right and from violent Islamists—the SPLC scoured records maintained by Indiana State University and the University of Maryland's Global Terrorism Database, as well as SPLC's own roster of apparent domestic terror incidents. The survey included incidents that likely involved mental illness and arguably personal grudges, but that seemed to have an obvious political aspect. It covered terrorism inspired by antigovernment, Islamist and various forms of race or group hatred. And it encompassed both actual terror attacks and those which officials aborted.

The survey also included cases that were not terrorist plots per se, but major unplanned violence that occurred when authorities confronted volatile political extremists for any number of reasons—pulling them over for a traffic infraction or trying to serve a warrant, for instance. Less than a quarter of the incidents cited (a total of 14 cases) were unplanned and occurred after some unexpected run-in. The time span covered is an important one—from April 1, 2009, a few days before the Department of Homeland Security issued a prescient but ultimately controversial study warning of a "resurgence in radicalization and recruitment" on the extreme domestic right, through Feb. 1, 2015, press time. That span also very roughly corresponds to the period since Barack Obama took office in early 2009, a development that most analysts agree spurred rapid growth of the radical right.

One of the most noticeable results was the regularity of major violence or planned violence from domestic terrorists—one attack, on average, every 34 days. It's debatable how that compares to the 1990s, when the first wave of the antigovernment militia movement swept the country. One 2013 study, by West Point's Combating Terrorism Center, found that violence from the extreme right between 2000 and 2011 had surpassed that of the 1990s by a factor of four, but many experts agree that that seems exaggerated. What is certain is that domestic terrorism from all sources is endemic and shows no signs of abating.

The body count of victims during the 2009-2015 period is certainly less than that of the 1990s, but that is heavily skewed by Timothy McVeigh's murder of 168 people in the 1995 Oklahoma City bombing. If the Oklahoma victims are subtracted, it appears that the rate of killing has remained approximately the same throughout. The SPLC study found that 63 victims had been killed in 2009-2015 terrorist attacks, along with 16 assailants. Another recent study, from the public-private National Consortium for the Study of Terrorism and Responses to Terrorism, or START, counted 368 people murdered by far-right extremists between 1990 and 2013, including 50 law enforcement officers. Without the Oklahoma victims, the START study (which did not include jihadists) shows an average killing rate of almost nine victims a year, while the SPLC study (including jihadists) finds an annual rate of almost 11.

The impact of terrorist attacks, far more than that of most other crimes, goes way beyond the number of victims. Such attacks send shock waves through targeted communities—racial groups, sexual minorities, Jews, Muslims, police and so on—and also can result, as security is ramped up, in a real loss of daily freedoms.

Other findings that emerged from the SPLC survey:

- Almost half of the attacks during the period apparently were motivated by the ideology of the antigovernment "Patriot" movement, including "sovereign citizens," whose movement has been described by the FBI as "domestic terrorist." A little more than that (51%) came from ideologies of hate, ranging from white supremacy to misogyny to radical Islamism.
- Of the 61 incidents where the weapon used is known, 59% of attackers used firearms, while 25% used explosives, including such jury-rigged bombs as propane tanks. Five percent used both firearms and explosives. And 11% used other weapons, including arson fires and a private plane.
- Attackers were overwhelmingly male, with just seven female assailants.
- Attackers were much older as a group than most violent criminals. Various studies have shown definitively that males aged 15 to 24 are responsible for a vastly disproportionate share of violent crime. In the case of the perpetrators surveyed in this study, only about 33% of the 87 whose ages are known were under the age of 29, with the remainder over 30. Aside from the 20 to 29 age group, the offenders were clustered most heavily between 30 and 49 years of age, although a surprising number were older than that. This suggests that perpetrators spend many years on the radical right, absorbing extremist ideology, before finally acting out violently.

The very high percentage of lone wolf and leaderless attacks and the declining number of groups on the radical right might suggest to some that the importance of the larger radical milieu is declining. But in fact, the groups and their ideologues provide the essential ideology that motivates the lone wolves and others. Today, that ideology is far less likely to come in publications or at group meetings. Instead, it lives on the Internet, always available and always dangerous.

The Theory of Leaderless Violence

In April 1987, a federal grand jury in Arkansas indicted 14 of the best-known white supremacist leaders in the United States for conspiring to overthrow the federal government. The men were accused of plotting to kill a federal judge and establish an all-white nation in the Pacific Northwest. They were also accused of conspiring, during an Aryan World Congress in northern Idaho in 1983, to help launch The Order, a violent terrorist group composed of more than 20 people that was finally smashed in 1984, when its leader was killed by the FBI.

The 1988 trial was a fiasco. Most observers agreed that prosecutors had failed to prove a conspiracy, and in any event an all-white jury acquitted all 14 men in what amounted to a disaster for the government. The defendants emerged as heroes to the radical right—but one of them saw a critical lesson for the future.

Pondering the case later, Louis Beam, a violent Klansman and movement theoretician, republished an influential essay on "leaderless resistance" he'd written in 1983. In it, he advocated the end of large groups with a pyramid leadership structure, arguing that such organizations were too easy to infiltrate and destroy. In their place, he called for lone wolf action or leaderless resistance, by which he meant cells of no more than six men. The idea was these cells and individuals would act on their own, with no direction or contact with other radicals. In that way, he reasoned, even the destruction of a single cell would have little effect on the larger movement.

"As honest men who have banded together into groups or associations of a political or religious nature are falsely labeled 'domestic terrorists' or 'cultists' and suppressed," he wrote, "it will become necessary to consider other methods of organization—or as the case may very call for: non-organization."

Tom Metzger, a prominent neo-Nazi who long operated from California but now lives in Indiana, took up the leaderless banner after Beam, tirelessly promoting his ideas with such publications as his "Laws for the Lone Wolf," carried on his Resist. com website.

Metzger advised fellow racists to avoid membership in groups, keep cash on hand for emergencies, and "never truly admit to anything."

"Never keep any records of your activities that can connect you to the activity," he wrote as part of a raft of suggestions. "Keep in mind that repeated activity in one area will lead to increased attention to the area and possibly to you. The more you change your tactics, the more effective you will become."

Whether because of the admonitions of Beam, Metzger and others, or simply because the tactic makes obvious operational sense, there is little question that the vast majority of recent terror attacks in the United States have been by lone wolves or very small leaderless cells. There's also little question that the political violence is continuing apace and that little seems to have been effective in stopping it.

It may not have had to be this bad.

DHS Weighs In, Then Out

On April 7, 2009, the team of Department of Homeland Security analysts who study non-Islamic domestic terrorism issued a confidential report to law enforcement agencies entitled "Rightwing Extremism: Current Economic and Political Climate Fueling Resurgence in Radicalization and Recruitment." The report, which noted the effect the economy and the election of the nation's first black president was having on the radical right, was almost immediately leaked to the right-wing media.

There, it was pilloried, with right-wing pundits and groups like the American Legion falsely claiming that it attacked military veterans, conservatives and others on the political right. That was clearly not true—in fact, the report was remarkably accurate in its analysis and warnings (which included the assertion that the threat of lone wolves and small cells was growing)—but enough of a political firestorm was created that then-DHS Secretary Janet Napolitano renounced its findings. The team that wrote it and lead analyst Daryl Johnson were falsely accused of failing to follow DHS' procedures and were criticized by Napolitano and others in public.

But then undeniable reality began to kick in.

Even before the DHS report's publication—three days earlier, to be exact—the evidence was mounting. On April 4, 2009, Richard Poplowski, an extremist who believed the government was about to unleash troops against American citizens, ambushed and killed three Pittsburgh police officers responding to Poplowski's mother's call reporting a domestic disturbance at her home. Poplowski, who also had racist and anti-Semitic views, was eventually sentenced to death in the killings.

Three weeks later, a Florida National Guardsman named Joshua Cartwright, who had earlier expressed interest in joining a militia group and also was "severely disturbed" about Obama's election, shot two Okaloosa County sheriff's deputies to death as they attempted to arrest Cartwright on domestic violence charges.

About a month after that, on May 31—after Napolitano had withdrawn the April DHS report and apologized for its contents—an anti-abortion activist who had also been involved in the antigovernment "freemen" movement of the 1990s shot and killed Kansas abortion provider Dr. George Tiller in Tiller's church. A few days later, on June 10, an elderly neo-Nazi named James von Brunn opened fire at the U.S. Holocaust Memorial Museum and killed a guard. He clearly intended to get into the museum and kill many more, but was himself shot and later died.

From there, the roster of human carnage continued without pause. A nativist extremist murdered a Latino man and his 9-year-old daughter; a longtime white supremacist was indicted and later convicted of sending a mail bomb that injured a diversity officer in Arizona; an angry tax protester flew an airplane into an Austin IRS building, killing himself and an IRS manager and injuring 13 others.

The Federal Response

But by then, almost the entire DHS team led by Daryl Johnson had left, discouraged by their treatment and DHS' new reluctance to issue any reports because of the fear that they might become controversial. They were exhausted and perplexed by the criticisms of Napolitano, who accused them of violating vetting procedures. And Napolitano was not the only political figure that criticized Johnson and his colleagues. Then-House Minority Leader John Boehner (R-Ohio), for instance, described the DHS report as "offensive and unacceptable" and charged, without any basis, that DHS had abandoned the word "terrorist" to describe Al Qaeda and instead was using "the same term to describe American citizens who disagree with the direction Washington Democrats are taking our nation."

In the years since then, the DHS has held up or canceled a number of planned reports on domestic terrorism of various types. Even some law enforcement briefings were cancelled. At the same time, in the aftermath of the Sept. 11, 2001, Al Qaeda attacks, the Justice Department's Domestic Terrorism Executive Committee was allowed to go fallow for more than a decade. But in the aftermath of the April 2014 murder of three people at two Kansas Jewish institutions, allegedly by a well-known neo-Nazi, Attorney General Eric Holder announced that he was bringing the committee back to life. It had held no meetings, however, as of press time.

Johnson's DHS unit was not a law enforcement agency, but it did play a key role in providing law enforcement with intelligence assessments. While it certainly could not prevent most terrorist attacks, the information it once produced was of high interest and importance to many police agencies. Former West Memphis, Ark., Police Chief Bob Paudert, whose police officer son was murdered by a father-and-son team of antigovernment extremists in 2010, has denounced the government for failing to brief police on such things as the "sovereign citizens" movement. His son's killers were sovereigns, who reject the laws of the federal government, and Paudert believes that if his son had been briefed on them he might have lived.

The FBI has taken up some of the slack left by DHS with occasional reports on extremism. And more than 70 fusion centers—regional centers where federal, state and local law enforcement agencies share information about threats—put out occasional papers and warnings to possible targets. But those who study terrorism are still deeply worried by the virtual dissolution of the DHS team. "It was a big mistake to take those people off the radar," said Mark Hamm, a criminologist at Indiana State University. "As soon as Barack Obama was elected, we could almost see it in the wind that there was going to be a revival of the radical right."

Still, there does seem to be some new activity on the part of the federal government, including the planned reactivation of the Domestic Terrorism Executive Committee. The government is funding a number of studies on radicalization and other matters related to domestic terrorism. But it still remains to be seen if these initiatives and others really deal effectively with the threat.

For his part, Daryl Johnson, who warned in 2009 of the increasing move toward lone wolf and leaderless terrorism—criminal acts that are almost impossible to stop in advance because so few people are involved in their planning—worries that the government still concentrates too much on foreign Muslim extremists, and that the recent Charlie Hebdo attack in Paris could add to that bias. He says that another extreme-right attack on the order of Oklahoma City, which was facilitated by the fact that only four people knew of the plot in advance, is entirely likely.

"We're long overdue for a much greater attack from the far right," Johnson said as he weighed the prospects for violence by terrorists like Larry McQuilliams, who clearly intended to kill as many people as possible. "We are long overdue."

10

Domestic Terrorism Isn't a Crime in Itself

Jenna McLaughlin

Jenna McLaughlin is a reporter and blogger who covers surveillance and national security for the Intercept. *She has also published articles for the* National Journal *and has previously worked at* Mother Jones, Baltimore City Paper, *and* DC Magazine.

On June 17, 2015, twenty-one-year-old Dylann Roof entered the Emanuel African Methodist Episcopal Church in Charleston, South Carolina, and shot and killed nine African American parishioners. The US Department of Justice charged Roof with murder in the commission of a hate crime, but the term "terrorism" or "domestic terrorism" was not included in the indictment. Many have been dismayed with what they view as a lessening of the severity of Roof's crime, but McLaughlin shows how domestic terrorism is not a crime in itself—and perhaps shouldn't be.

The Department of Justice charged Dylann Roof, the white 21-year-old man who allegedly gunned down nine black churchgoers in Charleston, South Carolina on June 17, with murder, attempted murder and use of a firearm, all in the commission of a hate crime. Attorney General Loretta Lynch announced the charges on Wednesday afternoon.

But the DOJ did not charge Roof with domestic terrorism, or include terrorism in the indictment.

"Why Wasn't Dylann Roof Charged with Terrorism?" Jenna McLaughlin, July 23, 2015, Reprinted with permission of *The Intercept*, First Look Media, Inc.

Some media outlets, lawyers, public figures and activists have called for Roof to be charged not just with a hate crime, an illegal act "motivated in whole or in part by an offender's bias," but with the separate label of domestic terrorism. Critics contend that the label of terrorism is too often only applied to Islamic extremists, and not white supremacists or anti-government anarchists. Many were outraged after FBI Director James Comey balked at the term during a June 20 press conference, telling reporters he didn't see the murders "as a political act," a requirement he designated as necessary for terrorism.

Roof's crime certainly seems to fit the federal description of domestic terrorism, which the FBI defines as "activities ... [that] involve acts dangerous to human life that violate federal or state law ... appear intended to (i) intimidate or coerce a civilian population, (ii) to influence the policy of a government by intimidation or coercion; or (iii) to affect the conduct of a government by mass destruction, assassination, or kidnapping."

Remember: Roof allegedly told a few friends that he intended the murder of the parishioners, attendees of historically black Emmanuel African Methodist Episcopal Church, to "start a race war," while his online "manifesto," verified by the FBI, confirmed his motivations to intimidate and assassinate. He took as inspiration, among other things, George Zimmerman's 2012 shooting of Trayvon Martin, the Confederate flag, the KKK and skinheads.

It turns out there was one major obstacle in charging Roof with domestic terrorism: The crime does not exist.

"As you know, there is no specific domestic terrorism statute," said Lynch during the press conference to announce Roof's indictment.

Even when the USA Patriot Act, post 9/11, redefined terrorism to include domestic crimes, the provision simply allowed the government to investigate more broadly what it called "terrorism." Actually charging someone with domestic terrorism remains a separate matter. Even criminals who use bombs or send money to ISIS—or Boston Marathon bomber Dzhokhar Tsarnaev—are not charged with the crime of terrorism.

Because Tsarnaev used bombs, the 30 federal charges against him—unlike Roof's case—included charges of "using a weapon of mass destruction," which is one of the few crimes specified in the U.S. criminal code section for terrorism. So it was accurate to say he was charged as a terrorist.

But shootings, regardless of motivation, intention or number of deaths, likely don't count. "It doesn't seem like a shooting would fit," says Faiza Patel, co-director of the Brennan Center's Liberty and National Security Program. "Or else a lot of crime would get caught up" in the terrorism net, she tells me.

There are, however, "aggravating factors" to be considered during sentencing, which prosecutors usually list on a formal indictment, and which can be used to determine whether the death penalty is justified, and those include "substantial planning and premeditation," to"cause the death of a person" or "commit an act of terrorism."

In Roof's case, the DOJ did not mention terrorism as an aggravating factor, but did reference "substantial planning and premeditation to cause the death of a person" for several of his charges. "When a prosecutor is writing an indictment, that's what he or she has to prove at trial," explains Michael German, a former FBI domestic terrorism investigator who now also works in the Brennan Center's Liberty and National Security Department. "Rather than making a complex argument [and] getting into a big discussion on what terrorism is, they'll make a simple argument."

Lynch did not explain why "terrorism" was not listed as an aggravating factor in Roof's indictment, though she did emphasize that the DOJ views hate crimes as "the original domestic terrorism." She noted that Roof's case, including his "discriminatory views towards African Americans" and his decision to target "parishioners at worship," made his crime a clear-cut case of a federal hate crime.

Courts can also apply a "terrorism enhancement," created in the mid-1990s, after sentencing, which would allow them to increase the penalty for the crime. This, writes Wadie E. Said, a law professor at the University of South Carolina, "also affords prosecutors and courts a vehicle of an expressive nature, to comment on their deep disapproval and condemnation of terrorism in a general sense."

Mike German believes that even the enhancement could be "questionable" in Roof's case. "If it had been a federal building rather than a church, a pipe bomb and not a gun ..." he says. "It's not distinguished by ideology, it's distinguished by the nature of the crime. But I don't have all the evidence."

Some white supremacists have been charged with the terrorism enhancement in the past. In 2010, for example, neo-Nazi Wayde Lynn Kurt plotted an attack involving assassinating President Obama in Spokane, Washington, which he described as the "final solution," and federal prosecutors added the enhancement to his sentence successfully.

For German and others, the issue is more about the importance of placing Roof's crime against African American churchgoers in the realm of terrorism alongside radical Islamists and ISIS. "Calling it a hate crime instead of terrorism seems to suggest it's less serious," he says. "Rhetoric is important." Patel echoes this notion: "It's more of a question of the narrative of the issue. If you call what he did terrorism, you connect it to the broader definition of acts of terrorism."

In general, however, Patel cautions against creating a specific domestic terror charge, because there are already too many crimes being labeled as terrorism that may be nonviolent or exercising freedom of speech. "You have all these acts that are terrorist but already criminalized," she says. "[The crime of] providing material support to a foreign terror organization is already problematic. It captures things that are nonviolent." And that, she believes, "comes close to the line of the first amendment."

Lynch was asked whether or not there should be a federal domestic terrorism penalty to help bridge the gap between crimes like the shooting of five military personnel in Chatanooga, Tennessee—which was immediately branded as terrorism, by law enforcement and media alike—and Roof's case, which was not. Lynch acknowledged the argument that leaving out the word terrorism may cause people to feel like the government "doesn't consider those crimes as serious."

But she doesn't agree. "I want to be clear that nothing could be farther from the truth. This type of crime in particular, racially motivated violence for which a federal law was specifically enacted to cover, is of grave importance. ... Sometimes people like to focus on the terminology. Since 9/11 there has been a great focus on [terrorism.] But it should in no way signify that this particular murder or any federal crime is of lesser significance."

11

US Domestic Terrorism Is Not the Threat It Is Made Out to Be by the American Media

Eric Vought

Eric Vought is commander of the Lawrence County Sheriff's Auxiliary in Michigan, including its intelligence section. He is a long-time political activist and freelance writer who has often written on civil liberties and Constitutional government.

In this excerpt, Vought argues that domestic terrorism is certainly a "cause for concern," although it is not the imminent threat it is usually made out to be by the American media. But this doesn't mean that law enforcement and intelligence communities in the United States can ignore the problem. Rather, they should concentrate their efforts on terrorist organizations' recruitment via social media and understanding the cultural dynamics that drive radicalization. Vought also suggests a reporting system whereby terrorist "indicators" can be dealt with before attacks. Like others included in this text, Vought points to the fact that many terrorists convert to Islam during the process of radicalization and that the best way to prevent such attacks is to build trust between law enforcement and communities.

Abstract

An overview of US domestic terrorism trends, concentrating on 1995 to present, graphs, discussion, and resources for further exploration. This working paper is intended as an introduction for either local law enforcement or the public and relies only on open source information. Some data on effective policing techniques, the impact of social media and Islamic State of Iraq and Syria (ISIS) recruiting, and possible future trends are included. Although the threat from terrorism is quite real, the trends will show that it is not a catastrophic one and that traditional policing techniques and Suspicious Activity Reporting (SAR) from the community can be effective in identifying threats. A background in criminal intelligence or terrorism is not assumed, but the citations should provide material for more advanced professionals.

1.3 Overview

Recent Events Focused Attention

- Paris Attacks[1], San Bernardino[2], Orlando[3] caught public attention;
- ~40% of Americans think we are losing 'War on Terror'[4];
- Question why counterterrorism tactics *do not seem to be* working;
- What is the terror threat? Are we countering it effectively?

Though the recent terrorist attacks in San Bernardino and Paris have brought terrorism home for Americans, most people still do not understand what is happening and why current anti-terrorism practices aren't (or rather, *do not seem to be be*) working. As the Commander of the Lawrence County Sheriff's Auxiliary and an intelligence analyst who worked with Air Force Studies and Analyses at the Pentagon straight out of college, I have addressed an international audience on active shooter situations and provided intelligence that brought federal attention to subversive groups operating within our state. My most recent task has been to prepare a talk (through the Sheriff's Office) on the The Islamic State of Iraq and Syria (ISIS)[5] threat and have developed a series of working papers based on that research.

This Presentation

- US domestic terrorism 1995 – 2016;
- How common is it?
- How do we detect it?
- What are current trends?
- How is ISIS different?
- How is social media impacting terrorism recruitment?

Covering US domestic terrorism trends from 1995 to present, this working paper places the current events into perspective, setting a foundation for effective policing techniques, the impact of social media on ISIS recruiting efforts and possible future trends in terrorism. Although the threat from terrorism is quite real, the trends show that it is not a catastrophic one. A combination of community awareness and traditional policing techniques are effective in identifying threats. Because a background in criminal intelligence or terrorism is not assumed, citations provide material for more informed readers.

This is the first in a series of papers related to these public briefings. Others will cover specific issues, including social media, the demographics of terrorism, and the role of the community, in greater depth. With ~40% of Americans feeling that we are losing the war on terrorism (ORC International 2015 and Rasmussen 2016) and a recent Gallup poll showing that terrorism is the top issue on the public mind [Riffkin, 2015], this is is the time to confront the facts.

What US Domestic Terrorism Looks Like

- US Terrorism is not common;
- Large, casualty causing events are rare;
- US jihadists are ethnically and racially diverse;
- There **are** concerning trends we need to watch carefully;
- Community awareness and traditional policing techniques **are** effective;

Contrary to public misconceptions, US terrorism is not common, large casualty-causing events are rare, and recent data shows that the average jihadist plot in America is developed by an ethnically and racially diverse group of mainly US citizens with only a few common patterns. There are, however, concerning trends. These data and their implications are addressed here.

2 What is Terrorism?

Many definitions

- UN, US agency, academic definitions often conflict;
- Looking at statistics, need to know how they mean it;

Definition 1 (Terrorism).

Not just violence, but *campaign of violence for ideological purpose*;

If we are going to discuss terrorism trends, we should start with defining what we mean by 'terrorism'. Unfortunately, many conflicting definitions are used and US agencies in particular often do not agree on a definition. The overall definition we would like to focus on is the 3rd Academic Consensus Definition of Terrorism (ACDT):

ACDT 2011

Terrorism refers on the one hand to a doctrine about the presumed effectiveness of a special form or tactic of fear-generating, coercive political violence and, on the other hand, to a conspiratorial practice of calculated, demonstrative, direct violent action without legal or moral restraints, targeting mainly civilians and noncombatants, performed for its propagandistic and psychological effects on various audiences and conflict parties. – [Schmid, 2011, 86-87].

The point is that we are not simply talking about violent acts but violent acts directed toward a *political or ideological purpose* which the actors hope to accomplish by *causing terror* in people who are *not the direct victims*. By this definition, Columbine was a criminal act commited by a sociopath for no particular purpose, but the

Oklahoma City attacks, the Charleston Church shooting, and San Bernardino are all acts of terrorism serving different ideologies.

The Global Terrorism Database (GTD), which we will work from extensively in this report, uses three primary criteria, which map reasonably well to the ACDT, for identifying acts of terror:

Global Terrorism Database (GTD) Criteria

1. The violent act was aimed at attaining a political, economic, religious, or social goal;

2. The violent act included evidence of an intention to coerce, intimidate, or convey some other message to a larger audience (or audiences) other than the immediate victims; and

3. The violent act was outside the precepts of International HumanitarianLaw. [START 2015a]

In order for an incident to be included in the Global Terrorism Database, it must arguably meet *at least two* of these criteria.

3.1 Annual Terrorism Casualties

For US casualties due to domestic terrorism, we look at the Global Terrorism Database [START 2015b], produced by the University of Maryland's National Consortium for the Study of Terrorism and Responses to Terrorism (START)[6].

The GTD does not yet have 2016 data, so we add selected incidents from other sources for the current year. [...] Terrorism casaulties for most years are insignificant at this scale. Annual casualties and injuries are both frequently under 10 for the entire United States. The average over the period, including 9-11, is only 153 fatalities and 76 injuries per year, nationwide [...] or 0.072 deaths/injuries per 100,000 people (2015 pop. 320 million). Four years in this dataset, 2003, '04, '05 and '07, have no US injuries or fatalities considered to be acts of terrorism.

Overall, therefore, the threat of terrorism to individuals is extremely low and is, in particular, lower than practically every violent criminal threat we face in Southwest Missouri. Even as a generational catastrophe, the 9-11 incident is about the same size as the Pearl Harbor attack of 7 December 1941[7] and nothing comparable has happened in our 20 year period.

US Terror attacks from 1995 to 2015, as shown in Figure 3 [table omitted], are well-distributed from coast-to-coast. A small number of higher casualty attacks (9-11, West Texas, Boston Bombing, etc) are dominated by attacks with few or no casualties. Most of the historical attacks in and around Missouri […] have resulted in no casualties. The Missouri map is showing a smaller area and can afford more detail without clutter. We therefore show attacks from 1970 to 2015. The incident which appears in Springfield, MO is the firebombing of the Metropolitan Comminity Church in 1983 by the members of the Covent, Sword, and the Arm of the Lord (CSA), which resulted in no injuries. A similar attack against a Mosque in 2012 is shown in Joplin. Most of the remaining Incidents were in Kansas City or St. Louis.

3.2 Global Comparison

World Terrorism

- Only 2.6% of terrorism deaths from terrorism since 2000 in Western countries;
- 78% of deaths happened in Nigeria, Afghanistan, Pakistan, Syria;
- Global deaths in 2014 totaled 32,685, an 80% increase from 2013;
- Number of countries experiencing attacks on the rise;
- Most deaths in 2014 from Boko Haram (Nigeria), ISIS 2nd;

The Global Terrorism Index compiles annual statistical reports on world terrorism from the Global Terrorism Database. Including September 11, Western countries have only experienced 2.6% of the world deaths from terrorism since 2000. 78% of all deaths occurred in only five countries: Iraq, Nigeria, Afghanistan, Pakistan and Syria. Global deaths from terrorism in 2014 totaled 32,685, an 80% increase from 2013's 18,111, both the highest total and highest increase ever recorded [IEP 2015]. The number of countries experiencing attacks and experiencing more than 500 deaths also increased markedly in the 2014 Index. Globally, the organization responsible for the most deaths as of 2014 was not ISIS itself but Boko Haram, a Nigerian regional group with ties to ISIS. As of the time of this writing, recently released GTD data for 2015 shows "that terrorist attacks declined by 13% and deaths by 14%, following years of striking increases." [LaFree et al., 2016]

3.3 Yearly Incidents

Not All Incidents Have Casualties

- Hostage events;
- Hijackings;
- Law Enforcement intervenes:
- Failed bombings;
- etc.

There are many terrorism incidents in the Global Terrorism Database which do not generate casualties, often because they fail or do not hit their intended targets. Kidnapping, hijackings, and hostage taking may or not result in casualties.

Law Enforcement may stop an attack in progress. In order to be included in the GTD, an attack must at least be attempted; *plots which do not proceed to an attempt are not included.* We will discuss interrupted plots further on. […]

The high point […] is in 1995 at 62 incidents. There is a sharp drop after 2003 and a steady increase starting in 2011 (mainly related to Islamic extremism) which has not yet reached 2003 levels. Even 1995 is low, historically. Going back further in the data yields yearly counts of over 100 during the 1970s and 1980s primarily from the Cold War and Marxist extremism.

Why the Dip in 2003?

Fact 2. *Annual attacks from jihadi terrorism were single digits both before and after the Invasion of Iraq in 2003.*

The invasion of Iraq started in 2003. It may seem odd that terrorist attacks dropped sharply at this time, however, the number of attacks related to Islamic extremism is very low (single digits) *both before and after* 2003 and does not contribute to the change[8]. Rather, the higher number in the early portion of the graph is due to attacks against abortion-related facilities in the mid-late 90s. As abortion-related attacks declined, there was a cluster of attacks by animal rights and environmental extremists (by such groups as the Animal Liberation Front and Earth Liberation Front) which ended in 2003. [...] A substantial portion of the business and education facilities attacked during this period were lab and research facilities.

Given the recent increase in US casualties and attacks from Islamic extremism, the global activities of the Islamic State (ISIS), its threats to attack US citizens, it is reasonable to expect that we are at the beginning of another multiyear cluster of terrorist attacks. This is particularly true when we look at the trends in yearly *plots*.

3.4 Plots

Plots v Incidents

Definition 3 (plot). Plots are incidents which either occured or were planned/prepared.

A plot interrupted before it is attempted will not be included in the GTD.

- New America Foundation Homegrown Extremism Database compiles data on plots;
- 505 plots covering 2001-2016;

For data on plots, we go to the New America Foundation Homegrown Extremism Database [2016b]. At the time of this writing, this database summarizes 505 plots covering 2001-20169 [...] Plots are included if they either occurred or were planned

and resulted in criminal charges for terrorism or related crimes[10].
So, this dataset includes plots which were interrupted by law
enforcement which are not counted in the GTD.

It is immediately obvious […] that domestic jihadist plots
increased markedly after the Islamic State formally declared itself,
spiking sharply in 2009 and again in the last few years. Although
there is no reason to believe that the exponential curve starting
in 2012 can be projected into the future, changes in the way ISIS
is marketing and recruiting strongly support that overall growth
will continue. We will discuss these changes in section 5. Jihadist
v. Non-Jihadist

- Non-Jihadist plots low 2013-2015, but that could change;
- Non-jihadists caused 23 of 87 casualties in our 2015 data11 ;
- From 2002-2016, jihadists killed 95 v. 48 for right-wing
  extremists12;
- We cannot focus exclusively on jihadist threats;

Non-jihadist plots are at a historical low point at the moment
(2013-2015). Given that this number tends to vary greatly over
time, however, the possibility of non-Jihadi plots should not
be ignored. Non-jihadist plots account for 23 of the 87 killed/
wounded […] According to New America Foundation's [2016b]
data, jihadists killed 95 in domestic terror plots from 2002-2016
(therefore excluding 9-11, including the Orlando night club attack
2016) versus 48 for right-wing extremists.

Jihadist Plotters
Not all a domestic threat

Most US Jihadis (~3/4) are not plotting domestic attacks but
are attempting to defect or provide support to ISIS overseas;

- US jihadis ethnically diverse;
- Most not ethnically Arab;
- 40% are converts to Islam[13];
- Many young, most male;

Even if we could discount non-jihadist plots and concentrate our law enforcement efforts on Islamic extremism, it would not necessarily do us much good. Given that the numbers of plotters are tiny against overall numbers of, say, American Muslims of Arabic descent or Muslim immigrants, a correlation would be of limited help in separating threats from non-threats, but New America Foundation's data shows that jihadist plots are committed by an ethnically/racially diverse group, primarily US citizens, almost but not entirely male [...]. Studies concentrating on only recent years find that most plotters are not ethnically Arab and some 40% are *converts* to Islam[14] [CNS 2014; Vidino and Hughes 2015, pp ix].

It should also be noted from these sources that most of the ISIS supporters arrested *are not plotting attacks within the United States*; rather, some three fourths are attempting to provide support to ISIS overseas or to travel to Syria to join ISIS ("foreign fighter aspirants"). For emphasis, this data includes very surprising examples of jihadi extremists, such as a Midwestern white female Evangelistic Christian converting to join ISIS[Hall, 2015], and *those seemingly inexplicable cases are common*. Making easy assumptions about ISIS recruiting is dangerous.

One of the patterns which does appear in the datasets is that although recruiting is highly dispersed and facilitated by social media, there are often family relationships between ISIS adherents (8 of 56 in CNS [2014]). *Siblings will sometimes convert and plot together*, despite attempts by parents to shelter or protect them [e.g. Reitman, 2015]. This type of plot generates very tight communication loops which can be difficult to discover or surveil. ISIS recruiting will often target youth who are 'lost', rebellious, and impressionable[Vidino and Hughes, 2015]. Often, but not always, the plotters will adopt a fundamentalist dress and appearance or otherwise abruptly change associations and social habits during radicalization.

4 How Do We Discover Terrorist Plots?

The New America Foundation dataset includes data on how we discover active plots. [...] Of those plots which were prevented and where it is clear from the sources how they were initially uncovered, a significant number are covered by:

1. Suspicious Activity Reports
2. Community/Family Tip
3. Routine Law Enforcement

Local law enforcement and the local community are instrumental in handling all three. Although most attacks occur in urban areas, ISIS recruitment is occuring nationwide. Local rural efforts may notice foreign fighter recruitment or preparatory activities even if the threat is actually to a more populated area.

The Oklahoma City attack was conducted against a government facility in an urban area, but most of the preparation activity occured in rural areas far from the target. Some of this, such as suspicious activity surrounding the Ryder truck and loading of the explosives, was noticed by locals but not immediately reported or not recognized for its importance [Michel and Harbeck, 2001]. Particularly to the Southwest Missouri audience relevant to the Sheriff's Auxiliary and our mutual aid partners, the role of these community-centric methods cannot be overstated.

High-tech methods, such as NSA surveillance, account for very few of the discovered plots [...] Use of informants account for a significant portion. Some sources report that as much as 50% of these informant cases are federal stings and 30% are 'non-traditional stings' where the paid informant initiates, plans, and provides most of the resources for the plot. This latter category is highly controversial as far as their expense versus actual utility to counterterrorism[16], so the number of such plots in the data may obscure the value of the three community policing categories and more traditional criminal intelligence methods [Human RightsWatch 2014, pp 21-55].

The category of community/family tips also must be emphasized because it represents a difference between the threat from US ISIS radicalization and regional jihadi terrorist threats: that the extended family and community around the individual or small cell do not condone their behavior, are alarmed by it, and *often seek help*:

What's more—and this is the greatest difference from the circumstances of young Palestinians who take up diverse forms of intifada—the *Muslim parents of radicalized second-generation youth do not understand the revolt of their progeny*. More and more, as with the parents of converts, they try to prevent the radicalization of their children: *They call the police; if the children have left the country, they follow to try to bring them back*; they fear, with good reason, that the older children will draw in their younger siblings. Far from being the symbol of the radicalization of Muslim populations as a whole, the jihadis explode the generational gap, which is to say, quite simply, the family. – [Roy, 2016][emphasis mine]

The author in that article is speaking of ISIS activity among French youth, but the statement applies equally to many US cases, whether to plots involving Muslims or converts[17]. Roy also explains some of the reasons why these plots seem to cluster in either 2nd generation immigrants or non-Muslims but not frequently in either 1st or 3rd generation immigrants. If this pattern is accurate, the ISIS phenomenon is similar to how troubled youth were attracted to radical Marxist groups when that was the 'in' form of rebellion rather than something new and incomprehensible.

One of the key factors in gathering this kind of voluntary intelligence is that the families and communities must trust law enforcement. Without trust, the information dries up and the community as a whole is less safe [Human Rights Watch 2014, pp 3]. In Southwest Missouri, this Sheriff's Auxiliary has had some success using non-peace officer volunteers as a trusted intermediary between reluctant community intelligence sources and law enforcement.

If there is something new and incomprehensible (or at least that we are still working to comprehend) about the recent jihadi threat, it is the way that ISIS leverages social media for recruitment.

5 Recent Trends and Social Media

Types of Attacks

- 9/11 centrally planned/coordinated; plotters sent to carry out plan;
- *Shoe bomber, underwear bomber* trained overseas; planned and carried out attack;
- Most US attacks 'homegrown';
- Paris attacks hybrid: Syria ringmaster, coordinated/carried out by French/Belgian nationals[18];
- Social media makes hybrid attacks easier, plotters harder to find;

The 9-11 attacks were centrally planned and coordinated. The attacks were executed by foreign adversaries sent to the United States to carry it out as planned by the Al Qaeda Global Network. Most US plots involve little or no overseas coordination. Some US terror plots involve an attacker who may be trained overseas but who develops and executes the attack without central coordination (e.g. *the underwear bomber*, possibly Tashfeen Malik of the recent San Bernardino attack). Often the attack is entirely 'homegrown'. Even when the attacker is motivated by a foreign terror group, they develop and carry out the plan with little or no outside input. The 2015 Paris attacks may represent a new hybrid strategy where an attack is conceived by ISIS in Syria but carried out by mostly homegrown extremists with a high degree of autonomy [Jenkins, 2015].

Information on the Orlando nightclub attack (12 June 2016) is still sparse, but as of this writing, it does not appear that the attacker, Omar Mateen, coordinated with ISIS abroad [Landay and Hosenball, 2016].

ISIS and Social Media

- Include Facebook™, Twitter™, cell phones and mobile apps;
- ISIS much more media-savvy than Al Qaeda or Al Nusra;
- ISIS Twitter Census: ~46,000 supporter accounts[19];
- ISIS recruiters target specific demographics, groom recruits;
- Target socially-isolated individuals and isolate them further[20];

The use of social media networks (including applications like Twitter™ or Facebook™, often on cell phones or mobile devices) enables a dispersed planning model and dispersed recruitment at a level not possible with previous technology. ISIS has been particularly adept at leveraging multimedia, social networking tools, and socially-disaffected tech-savvy youth. ISIS propaganda is slick, professionally produced, and effectively targeted at specific language and cultural groups, particularly when compared to Al Qaeda and even modern Al Qaeda spin-offs (e.g. Al Nusra). ISIS recruiters invest substantial effort into grooming contacts. Recruiters often focus on specific types of prospects. It is this focused effort which, for instance, allows ISIS to convert both Christian youth to a radical Islamist cult in one step as readily as disaffected Muslim youth by exploiting specific attitudes, doubts, and questions of each demographic [Vidino and Hughes, 2015].

An effort at a rigorous census of ISIS-related Twitter activty estimated on the order of 46,000 ISIS-supporting accounts in October and November of 2014 [Berger and Morgan, 2015, pp 7]. This broad base of online support allows the organization to effectively distribute news, propaganda, and training materials without a physical footprint where the recruiting is occuring.

ISIS targets socially isolated individuals and the recruitment process is designed to isolate them further. Converts are directed not to join local mosques or connect with American Muslim communities and instructed to cut ties with the family and real-world social network they have [Callimachi, 2015]. The increased isolation serves both to deter discovery and to cut the recruit off from sources which might expose the extremist propaganda. This extremely successful use of social media is one of the reasons the demographics of jihadist plotters is unexpectedly diverse. This kind of networking will likely be a continuing characteristic of modern extremism: an approach other radical groups will likely adapt to exploit its opportunities.

Where does this lead?

- We expect other extremists to learn from ISIS;
- Social media is two-edged sword:
- We can track and discover active plots;
- We can use volunteer labor;
- Defectors sometimes help intercept potential recruits;
- Organizations hijack ISIS social media to counter narrative;

The intensive use of social media and networking, however, has drawbacks as well as advantages. […] **Use of social media often lets us discover and track active plots**, even incorporating volunteer labor in that effort. Defectors from ISIS have even been used to help steer the unwary away from being sucked in or to get early stage recruits help [Callimachi, 2015] and several organizations routinely hijack ISIS online conversations to counter the radical narrative.

6 Conclusion

"Perplexed, but not in despair"

- Media puts terror in 'terrorist';
- Trends are concerning, need to be watched;
- Community participation and routine law enforcement make a difference;
- Suspicious Activity Reporting;
- Gathering intelligence requires trust;
- We must understand and adapt to social media trends;

Although terrorism is a serious concern, US domestic terrorism is not the existential threat it is often made out to be. Current trends with jihadi activity, however, do show some cause for concern, particularly in the potential for continued increases in recruitment via social media and an accompanying dramatic increase in domestic plots. The ISIS threat, especially in Southwest Missouri, is one which is amenable to routine law enforcement and community-oriented policing if community involvement remains high and trust is maintained between potential intelligence sources and peace officers. A robust Suspicious Activity Reporting system is also necessary to recognize and respond to threat indicators in a timely fashion. In order to understand and respond to violent extremism, however, today's criminal intelligence must understand the advantages and disadvantages of social media and the cultural dynamics driving radicalization.

We are hard pressed on every side, but not crushed; perplexed, but not in despair; — 2 Corinthians 4:8

References

1 November 2015
2 December 2015
3 June 2016
4 ORC International [2015] and Rasmussen [2016]
5 Sometimes referred to elsewhere as ISIL or Daesh, the Islamic State of Iraq and Syria will be referred to as 'ISIS' in this work.
6 An introduction and overview of the Global Terrorism Database is given in LaFree and Dugan [2007].
7 2,335 U.S. servicemen killed, 1,143 wounded, [About.com, 2015]
8 Obviously, though small in number, a handful of attacks by Islamic extremists contributed to the majority of the casualties.
9 The data chosen for plots starts in 2001 partly because the process and legal environmentfor terrorism-related arrests dramatically changed after 9-11. Although the "material support"charge was available in law since 1993, it had rarely been used before the attack on the Twin Towers. After 9-11, it is used in the majority of arrests, afecting the numbers. Arrest statistics crossing this period are therefore less useful for our purposes.
10 The database also includes plots and criminals where the planners died without being charged but where it is reasonably certain from the data that a terrorist plot occurred.
11 See appendix.
12 New America Foundation [2016b]
13 CNS 2014; Vidino and Hughes 2015, pp ix
14 Many of these convert from another faith directly to extremist Islam, never developing a connection to mainstream Muslims. Sometimes this is facilitated by an ISIS recruiter online with even the profession of their faith happening in cyberspace (see Section 5). US prison conversions are also becoming more common.
16 not to mention civil rights concerns...
17 Marc Sageman [2008, pp 89-107] explains why radicalization rates of US Muslims are markedly different from most of Europe but often comparable to France. Note that the

Paris attackers did not come from France but from neighboring Belgium. Sageman also commentson the fact that we have a porous southern border but that the Mexican coyotes who control smuggling operations across it are not friendly to jihadists (pp 107). Europe's internal borders are highly porous.

18 Congressional Homeland Security Committee testimony [Jenkins, 2015]

19 [Berger and Morgan, 2015, pp 7]

20 [Callimachi, 2015]

12

Westerners Commit Many Terrorist Attacks in the Name of Islamic Jihad

Sebastian Rotella

Sebastian Rotella is an award-winning senior reporter at ProPublica and has won a Peabody Award, a Dart Center Award for Excellence in Coverage of Trauma, and an Urbino Press Award. He has also been nominated for an Emmy and was a Pulitzer Prize finalist for international reporting.

The Tsarnaev brothers, who orchestrated the 2013 Boston Marathon bombings, seemed well integrated into American society and showed few signs of Islamic radicalization. Just as with the 2004 bombings in Madrid, Spain, and the 2005 attacks in London, England, these perpetrators shocked their neighbors when they were revealed to have been guilty of serious terrorist attacks. This is a troublesome trend in terrorism, where young Muslim men who are also very Westernized adopt Islamic extremist beliefs and will go to any means necessary to draw attention to their aims.

As an eighth-grader in a Cambridge public school, suspected Boston Marathon bomber Dzhokhar Tsarnaev was quiet, friendly, spoke good English and seemed at home in his adopted country.

While hundreds of police officers pursued the 19-year-old during a nationally-televised rampage across Boston Friday,

"Boston Bombing Suspects Echo Home-Grown Terrorists in Madrid, London Attacks," Sebastian Rotella, April 19, 2013. Reprinted by permission.

a former classmate recounted memories of the refugee who, according to counterterror officials, became a U.S. citizen on an ironic date: Sept. 11, 2012.

The story of the Boston bombers, Dzhokhar Tsarnaev and his 26-year-old brother, Tamerlan, is still unfolding at high speed. Many aspects of the case, including the brothers' motivations, are not yet clear.

But a portrait began to emerge Friday based on ProPublica interviews with counterterror officials, the public statements of relatives and associates, and reports in the media.

Counterterror officials believe the brothers were Islamic extremists. And the information available so far suggests that they appeared to integrate well into U.S. society, yet slid into a spiral of Islamic radicalization with bloody results. The profile has similarities to the home-grown terrorists behind attacks in Madrid in 2004 and London in 2005, according to counterterror officials.

"He was always a nice kid," said Cam Blauchner, who attended middle school with Dzhokhar, in a telephone interview with ProPublica. "He was shy, but not in a creepy way. He was a sweet guy. We played soccer together. I knew he was from Chechnya, but he never talked about it. He never mentioned his religious affiliation. I didn't know he was Muslim."

At some point, however, Dzhokhar and his brother plunged into a subculture that is grimly familiar to counterterror agencies in Europe and, to a lesser but worrisome extent, the United States, officials said.

There are signs that the brothers showed interest in the conflict in Syria, which has drawn al Qaida fighters and other militants from across the Muslim world and Europe, according to a U.S. counterterror official. Like others interviewed for this story, the official requested anonymity because he was not authorized to discuss the ongoing case.

The brothers had viewed videos about the plight of Syrian Muslims, the official said. Syria is the latest hotspot on the world map of jihad. Holy warriors a decade ago were inspired by videos about brutal combat between jihadis and Russian troops in the brothers' family homeland: the predominantly Muslim region of Chechnya, a breeding ground for al Qaida fighters in the late 1990s and early 2000s.

Tamerlan had viewed a video titled "I Dedicate My Life to Jihad," according to a U.S. law enforcement official. The brothers also were apparently influenced by the online Inspire magazine, a slick English-language publication that plays a strong role in disseminating ideological tracts and bomb-making techniques to Western extremists, the U.S. counterterror official said.

"It's like London, it's like Madrid in the radicalization," the counterterror official said. "These guys were produced by the international jihadist machine. The biggest thing is they were individuals willing to die. They were committed. There was interest in events overseas affecting Muslims. And a lot of Internet activity—the things that everyone in the counterterror community worries about."

The brothers had traveled in recent years to Russia, officials said. Tamerlan returned via New York from a trip to Moscow in July 2012, according to a U.S. law enforcement official. But officials said nothing so far indicates recent travel to Chechnya, in southern Russia, or war zones where terrorist groups provide training and direction to Western recruits.

"The big question is, are they part of a bigger network or just two brothers who decided to do this and pulled it off on their own?" the law enforcement official said. The well-choreographed bombing, the preparation of multiple explosive devices and the ferocity with which the fugitives battled police could indicate overseas training, officials said.

Suspected Chechen terrorists have been arrested in alleged bomb plots in Denmark, France and Spain in recent years. The failed "underwear" bomber who tried to blow up a plane over Detroit in 2009 was trained and deployed by al Qaida in Yemen. Would-be bombers in plots against New York in 2009 and 2010 were directed by al Qaida and allied networks in Pakistan.

The brothers are ethnic Chechens whose family moved around the war-torn Caucuses region when the boys were young. Tamerlan was born in Dagestan, near Chechnya, and Dzhokhar in Kyrgyzstan, according to officials and media reports. They went as refugees to the United States, arriving separately, according to counterterror officials and televised statements by an uncle in Maryland.

Dzhokhar arrived in 2002 on a tourist visa, obtained permanent resident status in 2007 and became a citizen in 2012, officials said. Tamerlan was admitted as a refugee in 2003 and later became a permanent resident, officials said. Tamerlan has an arrest for domestic violence on his record, the law enforcement official said.

The family lived in Cambridge when Dzhokhar was in middle school at the Community Charter School of Cambridge, according to his classmate, Blauchner. Dzhokhar stood out in a mostly African-American student population, but he got along well with classmates at the school, which stresses academic rigor and strict discipline, according to Blauchner, now a sophomore at the University of Chicago.

Dzhokhar had long hair and was short, pale and thin when Blauchner knew him in seventh and eighth grade. The immigrant boy wore the school-mandated uniform of khaki pants and a white, black or red polo shirt. He often ate lunch in the cafeteria with Blauchner and friends of Ethiopian and Bengali descent.

Dzhokhar studied hard and stayed out of trouble, according to Blauchner, and went on to win a scholarship, according to media reports. He was a student at the University of Massachusetts Dartmouth, according to media reports.

"He never seemed disgruntled," Blauchner said. "He never seemed sad. We weren't the nerdy kids, but we were more into academics."

Although he has not seen Dzhokhar since they graduated from middle school, Blauchner said he recognized his former classmate from the photos made public by the FBI. Blauchner was stunned.

The frenzy after the Boston Marathon attacks recalls the aftermath of the bombings on public transport systems that killed

191 people in Madrid in 2004 and 52 people in London in 2005, as well as a failed bombing in London two weeks later.

Those cases similarly featured frantic manhunts, publicized photos of suspects, and chaotic and confused media reports.

In Madrid, police tracked down a group of suspects who died after a shootout when their booby-trapped hideout exploded, killing a police officer.

The profiles of the Madrid and London suspects resemble the information emerging about the Tsarnaev brothers. Spaniards and Britons were shocked to discover that the terrorists had grown up in their midst and benefited from the comfort of Western societies.

A Tunisian-born leader of the Madrid bombers had received a Spanish university scholarship and was a well-liked employee at a real estate agency.

A Moroccan-born leader spoke street Spanish, was known by the nicknames "El Chino" and "Mowgli," dealt drugs and zoomed around with his long-haired Spanish girlfriend on a motorcycle.

Several convicted bombers in the failed London attack had come to Britain as children thanks to generous asylum policies for refugees from East Africa. Three of the suicide bombers who died in the successful attack two weeks earlier were seemingly well-integrated, British-born sons of Pakistani immigrants.

Yet, despite their Western ways, the attackers in London and Madrid harbored deep hatreds and inflicted indiscriminate slaughter on their fellow citizens.

Young men from Muslim immigrant backgrounds who radicalize in the West get swept up in the seductive outlaw culture of jihad. They construct a new identity in which the struggles of their Muslim homelands, even if they do not know them well, play a powerful role and foment anger at the West.

Counterterror officials say a similar trajectory could explain why the Tsarnaev brothers designed an attack on families at a festive sporting event.

Whatever the motive turns out to be, the fact that the brothers spent years in Boston sheds light on their choice of target. They likely knew the significance of the marathon, the ebb and flow of the crowds during the race, the geography. It remains to be seen whether they considered the symbolism of the date: April 15 was both tax day and Patriots' Day, marking the first battles of the American Revolution.

The choice of the day led some counterterror officials in recent days to suspect that the bombers were American-born, extreme-right, antigovernment terrorists.

In reality, it appears the suspects were the mix that most worries law enforcement: longtime Americanized residents who know the society well, but have a profile enabling them to develop connections to Islamic extremist ideology, if not actual movements, overseas.

The Madrid bombers had strong ideological links to al Qaida, but carried out the attacks with minimal overseas training and direction. The London bombers, in contrast, communicated with al Qaida masterminds who provided training and directed them to their targets from Pakistan.

The results in both cases were devastating.

Now, U.S. intelligence officials are combing through files, intercepts and data bases to see if they had previous information on extremist activity of the Tsarnaev brothers. In Madrid, London and many other cases, the attackers had earlier surfaced on the radar screen of law enforcement.

That is not necessarily a scandal; it is simply the reality of the terrain of counterterrorism.

Updated Friday, April 19, 9:10 p.m.

The FBI interviewed Tamerlan Tsarnaev, the elder of the brothers suspected in the Boston bombings, in 2011, two U.S. law enforcement officials told ProPublica Friday evening. The FBI agents conducted the inquiry into suspected extremist or terrorist activity at the request of a Russian security agency, the officials said.

"Yes he was interviewed," a U.S. law enforcement official said. "Nothing derogatory came of it. We reported it back to the other agency, but never got anything as far as further communications from them. There was never any reason to do anything else."

Tsarnaev's mother has told media outlets that the FBI had contact with her about her son's potential involvement in extremism five years ago, but the law enforcement official said authorities were only aware of the inquiry in 2011. Other media outlets also reported the 2011 interview late Friday.

In past cases in the United States and overseas, law enforcement and intelligence agencies have identified, followed or investigated suspects who were later implicated in attacks or plots. Experts point out that security forces simply do not have enough personnel to constantly watch every potential extremist who comes to their attention. Hard decisions have to be made.

Cases that have brought criticism of U.S. authorities include the failure to more closely investigate leads about Maj. Nidal Hassan, the accused shooter in the 2009 Fort Hood massacre, and about David Coleman Headley, a central figure in the 2008 Mumbai attacks.

13

The FBI Must Keep Up with Changes in Domestic Terrorism

Dale L. Watson

Dale L. Watson is the former assistant director of the Counterterrorism Division of the FBI. He led the FBI investigation into both the September 11 terrorist attacks and the 2001 anthrax attacks. He retired from the FBI in 2002 and works as a consultant for Booz Allen Hamilton.

In this portion of testimony before the Senate Select Committee on Intelligence in February 2002, Watson outlines the shift in the terrorist threat facing the United States in the immediate aftermath of the September 11 attacks in 2001. In doing so, he gives a history of previous domestic terrorist attacks and their shifting nature from the 1990s to the early 2000s. Then, Watson focuses on practical steps the FBI has taken post-September 11 in order to address these threats. He concludes by stating that US intelligence agencies must continue to adapt in order to address terrorist threats in the United States—both from international and domestic terrorists.

Good morning Chairman Graham, Vice-Chairman Shelby and members of the committee. I am Dale Watson, the Executive Assistant Director of the FBI over counterterrorism and counterintelligence. I am pleased to have this opportunity to appear before your committee and I convey Director Mueller's regrets for not being able to be with you today. This morning

"The Terrorist Threat Confronting the United States," February 6, 2002.

I would like to discuss the domestic and international terrorist threat facing the United States and the measures the FBI is taking to address this threat.

The terrorist attack of September 11, 2001, marked a dramatic escalation in a trend toward more destructive terrorist attacks which began in the 1980s. Before the September 11 attack, the October 23, 1983 truck bombings of U.S. and French military barracks in Beirut, Lebanon, which claimed a total of 295 lives, stood as the most deadly act of terrorism. The attacks of September 11 produced casualty figures more than ten times higher than those of the 1983 barracks attacks.

The September 11 attack also reflected a trend toward more indiscriminate targeting among international terrorists. The vast majority of the more than 3,000 victims of the attack were civilians. In addition, the attack represented the first known case of suicide attacks carried out by international terrorists in the United States. The September 11 attack also marked the first successful act of international terrorism in the United States since the vehicle bombing of the World Trade Center in February 1993.

[…]

At the same time, the United States also faces significant challenges from domestic terrorists. In fact, between 1980 and 2000, the FBI recorded 335 incidents or suspected incidents of terrorism in this country. Of these, 247 were attributed to domestic terrorists, while 88 were determined to be international in nature.

Threats emanating from domestic and international terrorists will continue to represent a significant challenge to the United States for the foreseeable future. Further, as terrorists continue to refine and expand their methodologies, the threats they pose will become even greater.

Background

The FBI divides the terrorist threat facing the United States into two broad categories—domestic and international.

Domestic terrorism is the unlawful use, or threatened use, of violence by a group or individual based and operating entirely within the United States (or its territories) without foreign direction committed against persons or property to intimidate or coerce a government, the civilian population, or any segment thereof, in furtherance of political or social objectives.

International terrorism involves violent acts or acts dangerous to human life that are a violation of the criminal laws of the United States or any state, or that would be a criminal violation if committed within the jurisdiction of the United States or any state. Acts are intended to intimidate or coerce a civilian population, influence the policy of a government, or affect the conduct of a government. These acts transcend national boundaries in terms of the means by which they are accomplished, the persons they appear intended to intimidate, or the locale in which perpetrators operate.

As events during the past several years demonstrate, both domestic and international terrorist organizations represent threats to Americans within the borders of the United States.

During the past decade we have witnessed dramatic changes in the nature of the terrorist threat. In the 1990s, right-wing extremism overtook left-wing terrorism as the most dangerous domestic terrorist threat to the country. During the past several years, special interest extremism—as characterized by the Animal Liberation Front (ALF) and the Earth Liberation Front (ELF)—has emerged as a serious terrorist threat. The FBI estimates that ALF/ELF have committed approximately 600 criminal acts in the United States since 1996, resulting in damages in excess of 42 million dollars.

However, as the events of September 11 demonstrated with horrible clarity, the United States also confronts serious challenges from international terrorists. The transnational Al-Qaeda terrorist network headed by Usama Bin Laden has clearly emerged as the most urgent threat to U.S. interests. The evidence linking Al-Qaeda and Bin Laden to the attacks of September 11 is clear and irrefutable. The law enforcement and military response mounted by the United States has done much to weaken the organizational structure and capabilities of Al-Qaeda. Despite the military setbacks suffered by Al-Qaeda, however, it must continue to be viewed as a potent and highly capable terrorist network with cells around the world. As we hold this hearing, Al-Qaeda is clearly wounded, but not dead; down but not out.

The FBI has moved aggressively during the past decade to enhance its abilities to prevent and investigate acts of terrorism against U.S. interests wherever they are planned. The FBI operates 44 Legal Attache offices (Legats) in countries around the world to help ensure that investigative resources are in place to support the FBI's expanding focus on counterterrorism and international organized crime. In the 20 years since President Reagan designated the FBI as the lead agency for countering terrorism in the United States, Congress and the Executive Branch have taken important steps to enhance the federal government's counterterrorism capabilities. The FBI's counterterrorism responsibilities were expanded in 1984 and 1986, when Congress passed laws permitting the Bureau to exercise federal jurisdiction overseas when a U.S. national is murdered, assaulted, or taken hostage by terrorists, or when certain U.S. interests are attacked. Since the mid-1980s, the FBI has investigated more than 500 extraterritorial cases. In addition to the investigation into the September 11 attack, several other ongoing extraterritorial investigations rank among the FBI's most high profile cases, including our investigation into the 1996 bombing of Khobar Towers in Saudi Arabia, which killed 19 U.S. servicemen; the bombings of the U.S. Embassies in Kenya and Tanzania, which killed 12 Americans; and the bombing of the USS Cole, which claimed the lives of 17 U.S. sailors.

As evidenced by our enhanced ability to conduct counterterrorism investigations overseas, the evolution of the FBI's response to terrorism during the past decade reflects the changing dynamics of terrorism. In the direct aftermath of the 1993 World Trade Center bombing the FBI began to focus investigative attention on the then-emerging phenomenon of

Sunni extremism and its operational manifestation in the radical international jihad movement. This effort paid almost immediate dividends when investigators uncovered and thwarted a plot by a loosely affiliated group of international terrorists led by Shaykh Omar Abdel Rahman to bomb landmarks throughout New York City during the summer of 1993.

This morning, I would like to briefly discuss the current terrorist threat in the United States, as well as the FBI's efforts to address the threat posed by domestic and international terrorists.

Terrorist Threat in the United States

The threat of terrorism to the United States remains despite proactive law enforcement efforts and significant legislative counterterrorism initiatives. The overall level of terrorist-related acts in the United States declined in the early 1990s, when compared to figures for the 1970s and 1980s, but has increased steadily during the past five years. There were two terrorist acts recorded in the United States in 1995, three in 1996, four in 1997, five in 1995, 12 in 1999 and 8 in 2000 (FIGURES COMBINE TERRORIST INCIDENTS AND SUSPECTED TERRORIST INCIDENTS). While terrorist designations for the year 2001 are currently being finalized, one incident, the attack of September 11, produced higher casualty figures than all previous terrorist incidents in the United States combined. Relatively high numbers of terrorist plots prevented by law enforcement in recent years further underscore the continuing terrorist threat.

Domestic Terrorism

Domestic right-wing terrorist groups often adhere to the principles of racial supremacy and embrace antigovernment, antiregulatory beliefs. Generally, extremist right-wing groups engage in activity that is protected by constitutional guarantees of free speech and assembly. Law enforcement becomes involved when the volatile talk of these groups transgresses into unlawful action.

On the national level, formal right-wing hate groups, such as the National Alliance, the World Church of the Creator (WCOTC) and the Aryan Nations, represent a continuing terrorist threat. Although efforts have been made by some extremist groups to reduce openly racist rhetoric in order to appeal to a broader segment of the population and to focus increased attention on antigovernment sentiment, racism-based hatred remains an integral component of these groups' core orientations.

Right-wing groups continue to represent a serious terrorist threat. Two of the seven planned acts of terrorism prevented in 1999 were potentially large-scale, high-casualty attacks being planned by organized right-wing extremist groups.

The second category of domestic terrorists, left-wing groups, generally profess a revolutionary socialist doctrine and view themselves as protectors of the people against the "dehumanizing effects" of capitalism and imperialism. They aim to bring about change in the United States and believe that this change can be realized through revolution rather than through the established political process. From the 1960s to the 1980s, leftist-oriented extremist groups posed the most serious domestic terrorist threat to the United States. In the 1980s, however, the fortunes of the leftist movement changed dramatically as law enforcement dismantled the infrastructure of many of these groups, and the fall of communism in Eastern Europe deprived the movement of its ideological foundation and patronage.

Terrorist groups seeking to secure full Puerto Rican independence from the United States through violent means represent one of the remaining active vestiges of left-wing terrorism. While these groups believe that bombings alone will not result in change, they view these acts of terrorism as a means by which to draw attention to their desire for independence. During the 1970s and 1980s numerous leftist groups, including extremist Puerto Rican separatist groups such as the armed forces for Puerto Rican National Liberation (FALN—Fuerzas Armadas de Liberacion Nacional Puertorriquena), carried out bombings on the U.S.

mainland, primarily in and around New York City. However, just as the leftist threat in general declined dramatically throughout the 1990s, the threat posed by Puerto Rican extremist groups to mainland U.S. communities decreased during the past decade.

Acts of terrorism continue to be perpetrated, however, by violent separatists in Puerto Rico. As noted, three acts of terrorism and one suspected act of terrorism have taken place in various Puerto Rican locales during the past four years. These acts (including the March 31, 1998 bombing of a superaquaduct project in Arecibo, the bombings of bank offices in Rio Piedras and Santa Isabel in June 1998, and the bombing of a highway in Hato Rey in 1999) remain under investigation. The extremist Puerto Rican separatist group, Los Macheteros, is suspected in each of these attacks. The FBI has not recorded any acts of terrorism in Puerto Rico since 1999.

Anarchists and extremist socialist groups—many of which, such as the workers' world party, reclaim the streets, and carnival against capitalism, have an international presence—at times also represent a potential threat in the United States. For example, anarchists, operating individually and in groups, caused much of the damage during the 1999 WTO ministerial meeting in Seattle. The third category of domestic terrorism, special interest terrorism differs from traditional right-wing and left-wing terrorism in that extremist special interest groups seek to resolve specific issues, rather than effect widespread political change. Special interest extremists continue to conduct acts of politically motivated violence to force segments of society, including the general public, to change attitudes about issues considered important to their causes. These groups occupy the extreme fringes of animal rights, pro-life, environmental, anti-nuclear, and other movements. Some special interest extremists—most notably within the animal rights and environmental movements—have turned increasingly toward vandalism and terrorist activity in attempts to further their causes.

In recent years, the Animal Liberation Front (ALF)—an extremist animal rights movement—has become one of the most active extremist elements in the United States. Despite the destructive aspects of ALF's operations, its operational philosophy discourages acts that harm "any animal, human and nonhuman." Animal rights groups in the United States, including ALF, have generally adhered to this mandate. A distinct but related group, the Earth Liberation Front (ELF), claimed responsibility for the arson fires set at a Vail (Colorado) ski resort in October 1998, which caused 12 million dollars in damages. This incident remains under investigation. Seven terrorist incidents occurring in the United States during 2000 have been attributed to either ALF or ELF. Several additional acts committed during 2001 are currently being reviewed for possible designation as terrorist incidents.

[…]

Cyber / National Infrastructure

During the past several years the FBI had identified a wide array of cyber threats, ranging from defacement of web sites by juveniles to sophisticated intrusions sponsored by foreign powers. Some of these incidents pose more significant threats than others. The theft of national security information from a government agency or the interruption of electrical power to a major metropolitan area obviously would have greater consequences for national security, public safety, and the economy than the defacement of a website. But even the less serious categories have real consequences and, ultimately, can undermine public confidence in web-based commerce (E-commerce) and violate privacy or property rights. An attack (or "hack") on a web site that closes down an e-commerce site can have disastrous consequences for a web-based business. An intrusion that results in the theft of millions of credit card numbers from an online vendor can result in significant financial loss and, more broadly, reduce consumers' willingness to engage in e-commerce.

Beyond criminal threats, cyber space also faces a variety of significant national security threats, including increasing threats from terrorists.

Terrorist groups are increasingly using new information technology and the Internet to formulate plans, raise funds, spread propaganda, and engage in secure communications. Cyberterrorism—meaning the use of cyber tools to shut down critical national infrastructures (such as energy, transportation, or government operations) for the purpose of coercing or intimidating a government or civilian population—is clearly an emerging threat.

On January 16, 2002, the FBI disseminated an advisory via the National Law Enforcement Telecommunications System regarding possible attempts by terrorists to use U.S. municipal and state web sites to obtain information on local energy infrastructures, water reservoirs, dams, highly enriched uranium storage sites, and nuclear and gas facilities. Although the FBI possesses no specific threat information regarding these apparent intrusions, these types of activities on the part of terrorists pose serious challenges to our national security.

The FBI Response to Terrorism

The FBI has developed a strong response to the threats posed by domestic and international terrorism. Between fiscal years 1993 and 2003, the number of Special Agents dedicated to the FBI's counterterrorism programs grew by approximately 224 percent (to 1,669—nearly 16 percent of all FBI special agents). In recent years, the FBI has strengthened its counterterrorism program to enhance its abilities to carry out these objectives.

The FBI Counterterrorism Center

As you are aware, congressional appropriations have helped strengthen and expand the FBI's counterterrorism capabilities. To enhance its mission, the FBI centralized many specialized operational and analytical functions in the FBI Counterterrorism Center.

Established in 1996, the FBI Counterterrorism Center combats terrorism on three fronts: international terrorism operations both within the United States and in support of extraterritorial investigations, domestic terrorism operations, and countermeasures relating to both international and domestic terrorism.

Eighteen federal agencies maintain a regular presence in the center and participate in its daily operations. These agencies include the Central Intelligence Agency, the Secret Service, and the Department of State, among others. This multi-agency arrangement provides an unprecedented opportunity for information sharing, warning, and real-time intelligence analysis.

Interagency Cooperation

This sense of cooperation also has led to other important changes. During the past several years, the FBI and CIA have developed a closer working relationship that has strengthened the ability of each agency to respond to terrorist threats and has improved the ability of the U.S. government to respond to terrorist attacks that do occur.

An element of this cooperation is an ongoing exchange of personnel between the two agencies. Included among the CIA employees detailed to the FBI's Counterterrorism division is a veteran CIA case officer who serves as the Deputy Section Chief for International Terrorism. Likewise, FBI agents are detailed to the CIA, and a veteran special agent serves in a comparable position in the CIA's Counterterrorist center.

The National Infrastructure Protection Center

Created in 1998, the National Infrastructure Protection Center (NIPC) is an interagency center housed at FBI headquarters that serves as the focal point for the government's effort to warn of and respond to cyber intrusions, both domestic and international. NIPC programs have been established in each of the FBI's 56 field offices.

The FBI Laboratory

The FBI Laboratory division has developed a robust response capability to support counterterrorism investigations worldwide. The FBI's mobile crime laboratory provides the capability to collect and analyze a range of physical evidence on-scene, and has been deployed at major crime scenes, including the World Trade Center bombing, Khobar Towers, and the East African Embassy bombings. The mobile crime laboratory contains analytical instrumentation for rapid screening and triage of explosives and other trace evidence recovered at crime scenes.

The Laboratory also provides the capacity to rapidly respond to criminal acts involving the use of chemical or biological agents with the mobile, self-contained Fly Away Laboratory (FAL). The FAL consists of twelve suites of analytical instrumentation supported by an array of equipment which allows for safe collection of hazardous materials, sample preparation, storage, and analysis in a field setting. The major objectives of the mobile crime laboratory and the FAL are to enhance the safety of deployed personnel, generate leads through rapid analysis and screening, and to preserve evidence for further examination at the FBI Laboratory. In addition, the Laboratory has developed agreements with several other federal agencies for rapid and effective analysis of chemical, biological, and radiological materials. One partnership, the Laboratory Response Network, is supported by the Centers for Disease Control and Prevention and the Association of Public Health Laboratories for the analysis of biological agents.

Threat Warning

Because warning is critical to the prevention of terrorist acts, the FBI also has expanded the terrorist threat warning system first implemented in 1989. The system now reaches all aspects of the law enforcement and intelligence communities. Currently, sixty federal agencies and their subcomponents receive information via secure teletype through this system. The messages also are transmitted to all 56 FBI field offices and 44 Legats.

If threat information requires nationwide unclassified dissemination to all federal, state, and local law enforcement agencies, the FBI transmits messages via the National Law Enforcement Telecommunications System. In addition, the FBI disseminates threat information to security managers of thousands of U.S. commercial interests around the country through the Awareness of National Security Issues and Response (ANSIR) program. If warranted, the expanded NTWS also enables the FBI to communicate threat information directly to the American people.

On September 11, the FBI issued a nationwide terrorist threat advisory via the National Threat Warning System; this advisory is in place through March 11, 2002, unless extended by the FBI. Since the terrorist attack of September 11, the FBI has disseminated 37 warnings via the NTWS. The FBI also has issued over 40 be on the lookout (BOLO) alerts via the NLETS system. BOLO alerts provide the names of individuals who are of investigative interest to the FBI.

Through a 24-hour watch and other initiatives, the NIPC also has developed processes to ensure that it receives relevant information in real-time or near-real-time from all relevant sources, including the U.S. intelligence community, FBI criminal investigations, other federal agencies, the private sector, emerging intrusion detection systems, and open sources. This information is quickly evaluated to determine if a broad-scale attack is imminent or underway. If a chemical, biological, nuclear or radiological material is threatened, the FBI Weapons of Mass Destruction Operations Unit (WMDOU) conducts an interagency assessment to determine the credibility of the threat, utilizing subject matter experts and federal agencies with relevant authorities. Based on the credibility of the threat, the WMDOU will coordinate the appropriate response by federal assets. As a result of this analysis, the FBI can issue warnings using an array of mechanisms, and disseminate warnings to appropriate entities in the U.S. government and the private sector so that they can take immediate protective steps.

The Future

I would like to conclude by talking briefly about steps we can take to further strengthen our abilities to prevent and investigate terrorist activity.

Encryption

One of the most important of these steps involves the FBI's encryption initiative. Communication is central to any collaborative effort—including criminal conspiracies. Like most criminals, terrorists are naturally reluctant to put the details of their plots down on paper. Thus, they generally depend on oral or electronic communication to formulate the details of their terrorist activities.

Although the FBI, and the law enforcement community at large, fully supports the development and use of innovative technologies to ensure that the United States remains competitive in today's global market, we remain extremely concerned about the serious public safety threat posed by the proliferation and misuse of technologies that prevent law enforcement from gaining access to the plaintext of terrorist and/or serious criminal-related evidence obtained through either court-authorized electronic surveillance or the search and seizure of digital evidence.

The use of commercially available, non-recoverable encryption products by individuals engaged in terrorist and other serious criminal activity can effectively prevent law enforcement access to this critical evidence. Law enforcement's inability to gain access to the plaintext of encrypted communications and/or computer evidence in a timely manner seriously impairs our ability to successfully prevent and prosecute terrorist and/or other serious criminal acts.

This significant challenge to effective law enforcement poses grave and serious public safety consequences. Unless the FBI enhances its ability for gathering and processing computer data obtained through electronic surveillance, search and seizure of computer evidence, and its ability to gain access to the plain text of encrypted evidence, investigators and prosecutors will be denied timely access to valuable evidence that could be used to prevent and solve terrorist and other serious criminal acts.

Joint Terrorism Task Forces

Cooperation among law enforcement agencies at all levels represents an important component of a comprehensive response to terrorism. This cooperation assumes its most tangible operational form in the Joint Terrorism Task Forces that are authorized in 44 cities across the nation. These task forces are particularly well-suited to responding to terrorism because they combine the national and international investigative resources of the FBI with the street-level expertise of local law enforcement agencies. This cop-to-cop cooperation has proven highly successful in preventing several potential terrorist attacks. Perhaps the most notable cases have come from New York City, where the city's Joint Terrorism Task Force has been instrumental in thwarting two high-profile international terrorism plots—the series of bombings planned by Shaykh Rahman in 1993 and the attempted bombing of the New York City subway in 1997.

Not only were these plots prevented, but today, the conspirators who planned them sit in federal prisons thanks, in large part, to the comprehensive investigative work performed by the Joint Terrorism Task Force.

Given the success of the Joint Terrorism Task Force concept, the FBI has established 15 new JTTFs since the end of 1999. By the end of 2002 the FBI plans to have established or authorized JTTFs in each of its 56 field divisions. By integrating the investigative abilities of the FBI and local law enforcement agencies these task forces represent an effective response to the threats posed to U.S. communities by domestic and international terrorists.

Expansion of FBI Legats

The FBI's counterterrorism capabilities also have been enhanced by the expansion of our Legat offices around the world. These small offices can have a significant impact on the FBI's ability to track terrorist threats and bring investigative resources to bear on cases where quick response is critical. As I've mentioned, the FBI currently operates 44 such Legat offices. Many of these have opened within the past five years in areas of the world where identifiable threats to our national interests exist. We cannot escape the disquieting reality that in the 21st century, crime and terrorism are carried out on an international scale. The law enforcement response must match the threat. By expanding our first line of defense, we improve the ability of the United States to prevent attacks and respond quickly to those that do occur. Given the nature of the evolving terrorist threat and the destructive capabilities now available to terrorists, the American people deserve nothing less. The expansion of the number of FBI Legal Attache offices (Legats) around the world has enhanced the ability of the FBI to prevent, respond to, and investigate terrorist acts committed by international terrorists against U.S. interests worldwide. As evidenced by developments in the Embassy Bombing cases in East Africa, the ability to bring investigative resources to bear quickly in the aftermath of a terrorist act can have significant impact on our ability to identify those responsible. I encourage Congress to support our efforts to counter the international terrorist threat by continuing to support expansion of our Legat program.

Results

Improved analysis and operational capabilities combined with increased cooperation and integration have enhanced the FBI's ability to investigate and prevent acts of terrorism.

Dozens of domestic extremists have been indicted and prosecuted during the past ten years. Among these are Timothy McVeigh, who carried out the bombing of the Murrah Federal Building in Oklahoma City in 1995. McVeigh was executed in June 2001 for perpetrating the worst act of domestic terrorism ever conducted in the United States. More recently, on January 25, 2002, anti-abortion extremist Clayton Lee Waagner was given a combined sentence of over 30 years in prison for various theft and firearms violations. Waagner is also suspected of sending over 250 hoax anthrax letters to reproductive services clinics in October and November 2001.

During the past ten years, more than 60 subjects associated with international terrorism have been prosecuted in the United States. These include Ramzi Yousef, operational mastermind of the 1993 World Trade Center bombing and a plot to bomb U.S. airliners transiting the far east (convicted in May 1997); Tsutomu Shirosaki, Japanese Red Army member who fired rockets at the U.S. Embassy compound in Jakarta, Indonesia, in 1986 (convicted in November 1997); and Gazi-Abu Mezer and Lafi Khalil, extremists who, in 1997, nearly carried out a plan to bomb the New York City subway system (convicted in July 1998). Yousef and Shirosaki were among the 16 fugitives indicted for terrorist-related activities that have been rendered to the United States from overseas since 1987. The 1997 plot to bomb the New York subway was narrowly averted by the FBI/New York City Police Department Joint Terrorism Task Force.

On October 18, 2001, four Al-Qaeda members received life sentences for their roles in a conspiracy to kill Americans which resulted in the August 1998 embassy bombings in East Africa. Mohamed Rashed Daoud al-Owhali, Khalfan Khamis Mohamed, Wadih el-Hage, and Mohamed Sadeek Odeh were convicted earlier in 2001 in the Southern District of New York (SDNY) on a variety of charges related to the embassies bombing plot. Two other subjects in this case are awaiting trial in the SDNY.

In December 1999 the coordinated efforts of the FBI and other law enforcement/intelligence agencies were instrumental in responding to the millennium threat exposed when Ahmed Ressam was apprehended attempting to smuggle explosives across the U.S.-Canadian border near Seattle. On April 6, 2001, after a three-week trial in Los Angeles, Ressam was found guilty on all counts brought against him. On March 7, 2001, Abdelghani Meskini, another individual suspected of involvement in the plot to bomb the Los Angeles airport, had pled guilty in the Southern District of New York to charges of providing material support to Ressam. On July 13, 2001, a third suspect subject, Mokhtar Haouari, was convicted of charges related to the plot. In January of this year, Haouari was sentenced to 24 years in prison for his role in supporting Ressam's plot to carry out terrorist activity in the United States. One indicted subject, Abdelmajid Dahoumane, is in Algerian custody.

In addition, numerous individuals have been indicted for their involvement in terrorist activities and are currently being sought by the FBI. Usama Bin Laden and 15 other subjects stand indicted for their roles in Al-Qaeda and the 1998 U.S. embassy bombings in East Africa. Three additional subjects are in custody in the United Kingdom but are expected to be extradited soon to stand trial in the SDNY.

In October 2001 the FBI established the Most Wanted Terrorists program to focus expanded attention on indicted terrorist suspects. Usama Bin Laden was among the first 22 names placed on this list. In June 1998 Bin Laden had been named to the FBI's Top Ten Most Wanted Fugitives list.

Conclusion

Despite the current focus on international terrorism, it is important to remain cognizant of the full range of threats that confront the United States. These threats continue to include domestic and international terrorists. While the majority of attacks perpetrated by domestic terrorists have produced low casualty figures, the 169 lives claimed in the Oklahoma City bombing and the potential very heavy loss of lives that could have resulted from various thwarted plots demonstrate the interest among some domestic extremists in inflicting mass casualties.

On September 11, 2001, the scope and sophistication of the international radical jihad movement was demonstrated with horrendous clarity when 19 hijackers commandeered four commercial airliners, crashing two of them into the World Trade Center, one into the Pentagon, and the other into a remote field in Pennsylvania. This attack resulted in more casualties than any other terrorist act ever recorded.

[…]

Terrorism represents a continuing threat to the United States and a formidable challenge to the FBI. In response to this threat, the FBI has developed a broad-based counterterrorism program, based on robust investigations to disrupt terrorist activities, interagency cooperation, and effective warning. While this approach has yielded many successes, the dynamic nature of the terrorist threat demands that our capabilities continually be refined and adapted to continue to provide the most effective response.

14

US Law Enforcement Must Develop Relations with Muslim Communities

Toni Johnson

Toni Johnson is a staff writer and editor for the Council on Foreign Relations' website (cfr.org), where she mostly writes about foreign policy issues involving the United States. She spent four years as a reporter for Congressional Quarterly and received her master's degree in international journalism from American University.

In this article, Johnson asserts that homegrown Islamic radicals are not only a threat to the United States but have also committed—and will continue to commit—major terrorist attacks abroad. Given this threat, the US intelligence community must find new and better ways of preventing and/or monitoring potential homegrown terrorists. Based on a report for the American Security Project, Johnson explores how this might be done. One conclusion that she draws is that the US government needs to stop the "alienation cycle" in Muslim communities that feeds into radicalization. To do this, trust must be built between US government agencies and Muslim communities, and "heavy-handed" tactics that deny civil liberties must be avoided.

Introduction

The number of terror incidents involving Islamic radicals who are U.S. citizens has seen an uptick in recent years. U.S. citizens have also been involved in some high-profile international terrorism incidents, such as the 2008 attacks in Mumbai, India. This has prompted growing questions about motivations of Islamic radicals in the United States in the decade since the September 11, 2001, terror attacks by al-Qaeda that killed nearly three thousand people. As the list has grown, the question increasingly arises of how to combat Islamist terrorism at home. U.S. law enforcement intelligence is hampered by an underdeveloped relationship with Muslim communities and the inability to readily identify potential terrorists—especially since they often do not appear to need help from international organizations like al-Qaeda to carry out plots.

Islamic Radicalism in the United States

Between September 11, 2001, and the end of 2009, the U.S. government reported forty-six incidents of "domestic radicalization and recruitment to jihadist terrorism" that involved at least 125 people, according to a May 2010 Rand Corporation report. Half the cases involve single individuals, while the rest represent "tiny conspiracies," according to congressional testimony by Brian Michael Jenkins, author of the Rand report.

About one-quarter of the plots identified have links to major international jihadist groups like al-Qaeda, according to the Rand report. But a March 2010 Bipartisan Policy Center paper points out an increasing number of Americans are playing high-level operational roles in al-Qaeda and aligned groups, as well as a larger numbers of Americans who are attaching themselves to these groups.

There had been an average of six cases per year since 2001, but that rose to thirteen in 2009, a worrisome sign to some experts. Still, analysts caution against assuming any large-scale radicalization of the U.S. Muslim population. Cases of Muslims involved in domestic terror plots represent a very small minority of the entire U.S. Muslim community, which ranges somewhere between less than 2 million and upwards of 7 million (U.S. law forbids mandatory questions about religion on the U.S. Census [*WSJ*], and polling and other estimates have produced a wide range in population numbers.)

"Given the fact that we're dealing with such a miniscule minority of, in this case, the Muslim population, it's extremely difficult to craft national policies that affect the tiny minority, or as we would say, statistically detailed distribution," said Richard Falkenrath, a CFR adjunct senior fellow for counterterrorism and former New York City deputy commissioner for counterterrorism.

Sources of Radicalization

As of January 2010, all but two people arrested in the last decade for domestic terror connected to radical Islam have been male. Otherwise, at least three recent think tank reports have concluded that suspects follow no definitive ethnic or socioeconomic pattern, being both immigrant and native-born, and ranging in age from 18 to 70.

"The only common denominator appears to be a newfound hatred for their native or adopted country, a degree of dangerous malleability, and a religious fervor justifying or legitimizing violence that impels these very impressionable and perhaps easily influenced individuals toward potentially lethal acts of violence," argues a September 2010 paper by the Bipartisan Policy Center.

Counterterrorism experts point to online social media sites and charismatic English-speaking preachers, such Anwar al-Awlaki, as a boon for terrorist groups looking to spread their ideology in the United States. The U.S. prison system remains another concern (PBS) for jihadist recruiting. In January 2010, the Senate Foreign Relations Committee issued a report on al-Qaeda, which found that as many three dozen U.S. ex-convicts thought to have become radicalized in prison may have attended terrorist training camps in Yemen. In 2005, law enforcement officials foiled a plot to attack numerous sites in California by three Muslim men linked to Jamiyyat Ul Islam Is Saheeh, a militant, prison-based Muslim group started in 1997. A March 2010 FBI bulletin on radicalization in prison says more study is needed. "Authorities must temper their responses with the understanding that religious conversion differs from radicalization," the report says.

Major Terror Cases

Nearly all of the high-profile domestic terror incidents have resulted in convictions in U.S. federal courts. Here are profiles of major cases:

Domestic Terror

- **Jose Padilla.** A U.S. citizen on a flight from Pakistan, Padilla was detained in Chicago in 2002 and accused of participating in an al-Qaeda plot to detonate a "dirty bomb" on U.S. soil. Padilla, who converted to Islam while in jail, was labeled an "enemy combatant," held in a military prison, and denied access to civilian courts for over three years. In late 2005, as the Supreme Court was weighing the constitutionality of Padilla's detention, he was added to a federal criminal case of two other men accused of supplying money, supplies, and recruits for a North American support cell of Islamic extremists, unrelated to the alleged dirty bomb plot. Padilla was sentenced in 2008 to seventeen years in prison.
- **Detroit Sleeper Cell.** Six days after September 11, 2001, police raided an apartment in Detroit, found video footage of tourist sites like Disneyland and drawings that authorities alleged depicted a U.S. air base in Turkey and a military hospital in Jordan. Four legal immigrants, three from Morocco and one from Algeria, were accused of collecting intelligence for terrorist attacks. Three of the men were subsequently convicted, but the fourth was acquitted. The Justice Department later removed the lead prosecutor from the case, saying he knowingly withheld information that could have proved the group's innocence, which later led to reversal of the convictions.
- **Faisal Shahzad.** A naturalized U.S. citizen from Pakistan, Shahzad attempted to bomb New York's Times Square with a parked car full of explosives in May 2010. Shahzad was inspired by Pakistani militants and told authorities he was a "fan and follower" of radical cleric Anwar al-Awlaki, but appears to

have planned the bombing alone. He plead guilty and was sentenced to life in prison without the possibility of parole.

- **Nidal Hasan.** Virginia-born Muslim and career military psychiatrist Hasan shot and killed thirteen people and wounded nearly thirty in November 2009 at the Fort Hood Army base where he worked. Hasan followed Anwar al-Awlaki's lectures and sent twenty-one emails to him asking what Islamic law said about Muslim-American soldiers killing their colleagues. Awlaki responded twice. Hasan frequently argued that it was immoral for Muslim-American soldiers to fight against fellow Muslims in Iraq and Afghanistan, and found out he was being deployed shortly before his rampage. He will be tried in military court and an investigating officer has recommended capital punishment.

- **Lackawanna Six.** Nearly a year after September 11, six Yemeni-American childhood friends from a Buffalo, NY, suburb were arrested in what was a "showpiece for the Bush administration's war on terror" (*NYT*), and one of the first examples of preemptive justice on terrorism. They attended an al-Qaeda training camp in Kandahar in the spring of 2001, which some in the group claim was motivated by curiosity. All six plead guilty to providing material support for a terrorist organization and were sentenced to seven to nine years in prison. Some have been released, and three will be granted aliases by the U.S. government upon their release for testifying against al-Qaeda.

- **Fort Dix Plot.** Six foreign-born Muslims—including four ethnic Albanians from Macedonia and Kosovo who illegally immigrated, a Palestinian from Jordan turned U.S. citizen, and a legal Turkish immigrant—were arrested in 2007 for a plot targeting the Fort Dix Army base in New Jersey. The arrests were made after a store clerk turned in a video showing them shooting guns and calling for jihad. The group had no apparent connection with any international terror organizations. Five of the six received life prison sentences from a federal court in late 2008.

- **The Portland Seven.** This diverse group of American Muslims in Portland, OR, was charged with attempting to join al-Qaeda and levy war against the United States in a 2002 and 2003 fifteen-count federal indictment aided by the Patriot Act. One fugitive of the group joined al-Qaeda and was killed by Pakistani forces in Afghanistan. The remaining six are serving, or have served, prison time.

- **Mohamed Osman Mohamud.** Somali-born, naturalized U.S. citizen Mohamud penned several articles for the online magazine Jihad Recollections in 2009, and U.S. authorities allege he attempted to connect with terrorists in Pakistan. In November 2010, police arrested Mohamud in Portland, OR, for trying to detonate what he believed to be a car bomb during a Christmas-tree lighting ceremony. The bomb was actually a fake planted by the FBI, and some question whether the sting operation represented entrapment (*NYT*).

Terror Abroad

- **Anwar al-Awlaki.** New Mexico-born Anwar al-Awlaki was a radical Muslim cleric accused of recruiting for al-Qaeda who increasingly advocated violent jihad. Sometimes called the Osama bin Laden of the Internet, Awlaki corresponded primarily through cyberspace with Fort Hood-shooter Nidal Hasan, a Minnesota group that recruited for al-Shabaab, and three of the September 11 hijackers. His lectures were also mentioned by one of the men convicted in the Fort Dix plot, as well as would-be Times Square bomber Faisal Shahzad. In April 2010, the Obama administration authorized a targeted killing of Awlaki in Yemen. His father acquired two groups of human rights lawyers to challenge Awlaki's inclusion on a list of people to be killed without trial, but the administration's order was upheld by a federal judge in December 2010. Awlaki was reported killed in Yemen (CBS) on September 30, 2011, by a U.S. airstrike, which also killed U.S.-born Samir Khan, editor of an English-language al-Qaeda web magazine. The deaths have raised fresh concerns about constitutionality of such operations.

- **John Walker Lindh**. A native Californian, Lindh converted at a local mosque before traveling to Yemen, Pakistan, and Afghanistan to join the Taliban, and was captured in November 2001 as the U.S. military invaded Afghanistan. Due to a plea bargain, Lindh was sentenced to twenty years in prison by a federal court on the condition that he drop claims that he had been mistreated or tortured and that he not speak publicly about the conditions of his sentence.

- **David Headley.** A native of Washington, DC, Headley helped Pakistan-based group Lashkar-e-Taiba identify targets for the 2008 terrorist attacks in Mumbai. Headley was also plotting to attack the Copenhagen offices of the newspaper that published cartoons depicting the prophet Mohammad. After September 11, the Drug Enforcement Administration employed Headley as an informant in Pakistan, despite repeated warnings that he might be a terrorist. Headley plead guilty in 2010 in a U.S. federal court and faces life in prison.

- **Pakistan Five.** Five U.S. citizens who reached out to extremists through YouTube were arrested in Pakistan on their way to fight against U.S. troops in Afghanistan with a jihadist group. The young men of Pakistani, Egyptian, Ethiopian, and Eritrean decent—who attended the same northern Virginia mosque—maintain they traveled for a wedding and to help Muslims displaced by the war in Afghanistan. Pakistani courts sentenced them to ten years in prison.

- **Somalia Plot.** Fourteen Somali-Americans were charged in August 2010 with providing material support and recruits for al-Shabaab, an Islamic militant organization fighting an insurgency in Somalia. Of the group, most were in Somalia at the time of the indictment.

- **Shirwa Ahmed**. In October 2008, Shirwa Ahmed, a Somalia-born U.S. citizen, drove a car full of explosives into a government compound in northern Somalia, killing himself and more than twenty people. Speaking at the Council on Foreign Relations in February 2009, FBI Director Robert S. Mueller said Ahmed was radicalized in his Minnesota hometown of Minneapolis.

Policy Implications

An October 2010 report from the Washington, DC-based American Security Project suggests U.S. policy find strategies that address the "deep-seated perceptions and attitudes" among the Muslim and non-Muslim population that help "fuel the alienation cycle that has helped to make a small but increasing number of Americans more susceptible to extremist ideology."

Some experts say the government needs to do a better job with Muslim communities, perhaps their best source of intelligence on terrorist plots, and should avoid heavy-handed tactics and civil liberties abuses that jeopardize trust building. For example, following the 9/11 terrorist attacks, the FBI began routinely interviewing Arab and Muslim men in the country, which garnered criticism from civil liberties advocates that it unfairly targeted entire communities.

But engaging Muslim communities presents challenges. "The U.S. government runs major national programs, but it's not present in a serious, sustained way in all the communities of interest," says CFR's Falkenrath. "The only government agencies that really are [present] are the local agencies: health departments, education departments, police departments, fire departments. As a practical matter, if you really wanted to do something in this (what is called counter-radicalization), you'd need to find a way to incorporate the government agencies at the local level into such an effort."

Nadia Roumani, director of the American Muslim Civic Leadership Institute, also stresses the importance of coordinating among agencies. "Oftentimes, especially on this issue, there will be one strategy that's been taken by local law enforcement and a different strategy taken by the FBI and a different strategy taken by [the Department of Homeland Security]," she noted in a July 2010 panel discussion. "And then the community's confused [on] who to engage and how these are all connecting." Law experts Tara Lai Quinlan and Deborah Ramirez suggest developing a "nationally coordinated law enforcement-community partnership infrastructure" (HuffingtonPost) similar to what is being done to combat radicalism in the United Kingdom.

15

Domestic Terrorism Is a Relatively Small Problem

Larry Kummer

Larry Kummer is editor of Fabius Maximus and has over thirty-seven years experience in the financial industry. For twenty years, he actively worked for Republican political campaigns. He began writing about geopolitics at the Defense and the National Interest website in 2003.

Since 2001, US security agencies have been putting nearly all of their resources into rooting out homegrown Islamic terrorists. However, according to Kummer, these terrorists are so rare that they are most likely "manufactured" by the FBI. The American people and US security forces are less interested in the real threat: the ultra-conservative wing of the Republican party. These extremists (such as those involved in the Sovereign Citizens movement) might be plotting more attacks against the US states, but they are not taken seriously. According to Kummer, ordinary citizens and those in the security industry should not overblow the small threat of Islamic terrorists and, instead, should focus on the possible threat of right-wing groups in the United States.

Summary: Since 9/11 the security services have repeatedly warned about domestic terrorists of the Left and Right. The important conclusion from these—and the numbers—is that domestic terrorism is probably a relatively small problem, one that our security agencies might give too much attention. This diverts attention and burns resources that could go to bigger and more likely risks.

(1) Islamic terrorist attacks coming to the Homeland!

[In] July 2007 a summary was released of an National Intelligence Estimate about "The Terrorist Threat to the US Homeland." This alarming forecast proved quite wrong, but that has not slowed the gravy train to the security services. Excerpt:

> We judge the US Homeland will face a persistent and evolving terrorist threat over the next three years. The main threat comes from Islamic terrorist groups and cells, especially al-Qa'ida, driven by their undiminished intent to attack the Homeland and a continued effort by these terrorist groups to adapt and improve their capabilities.
>
> … We are concerned, however, that this level of international cooperation may wane as 9/11 becomes a more distant memory and perceptions of the threat diverge. … As a result, we judge that the United States currently is in a heightened threat environment.

(2) Rightwing extremists might attack the Homeland!

The DHS published an Assessment (not an NIE) on 7 April 2009 about "Rightwing Extremism: Current Economic and Political Climate Fueling Resurgence in Radicalization and Recruitment."

It was quickly leaked by those who did not want the government protecting us from such threats. the subject proved too hot for our leaders. Excerpt:

> The economic downturn and the election of the first African American president present unique drivers for rightwing radicalization and recruitment.
>
> … The current economic and political climate has some similarities to the 1990s when rightwing extremism experienced a resurgence fueled largely by an economic recession, criticism about the outsourcing of jobs, and the perceived threat to U.S. power and sovereignty by other foreign powers.

The possible passage of new restrictions on firearms and the return of military veterans facing significant challenges reintegrating into their communities could lead to the potential emergence of terrorist groups or lone wolf extremists capable of carrying out violent attacks.

Conservatives went wild in their condemnations. Here's a rebuttal to some of their claims. The Washington Times reported that Ms. Napolitano told the House Homeland Security Committee on 13 May 2009 (oddly the only paper I see reporting this):

> "The wheels came off the wagon because the vetting process was not followed. ... "The report is no longer out there. ... An employee sent it out without authorization. ... {It will be} replaced or redone in a much more useful and much more precise fashion."

Daryl Johnson, then a senior domestic terrorism analyst and co-author of the report, said that the government responded quickly to the critics, gutting the domestic terrorism unit. His interview is a must-read for anyone interested in the operation of our security services (illustrating their deep dysfunctionality).

Were they right? Look over the SPLC's comprehensive list of domestic terrorist plots and serious incidents since the 1995 Oklahoma City bombing.

(3) How do police rank domestic terror threats?

To assess the threat of domestic terrorism we can see the surveys of state and local law enforcement agencies by the U of Maryland's National Consortium for the Study of Terrorism and Responses to Terrorism, The threat rankings change rapidly over even a few years—unrelated to actual changes in the environment—showing that they're guessing about the likelihood of threats. See this excerpt from their 2014 report:

> ... law enforcement perceptions about what is a serious threat in their community has changed significantly over time. Law enforcement is much more concerned about sovereign citizens, Islamic extremists, and militia/patriot group members compared

to the fringe groups of the far right, including Christian Identity believers, reconstructed traditionalists (i.e., Odinists), idiosyncratic sectarians (i.e., survivalists), and members of doomsday cults.

... there was significant concern about the resurgence of the radical far right (as evidenced by the 2006-07 survey, as well as additional concerns raised after the 2008 election of President Barack Obama), but it appears as though law enforcement is, at present, less concerned about these groups. Such changing perceptions about what is a serious terrorist threat is an important finding because identifying and prioritizing a threat is akin to hitting a moving target and evolves as new intelligence, data, and events develop.

Perceived Threat of Extremists by Group

GROUP	POTENTIAL THREAT, 2013-14	POTENTIAL THREAT, 2006-07
Sovereign Citizens	3.20 (1)	2.49 (7)
Islamic Extremists/Jihadists	2.89 (2)	3.13 (1)
Militia/Patriot	2.67 (3)	2.61 (6)
Racist Skinheads	2.58 (4)	2.82 (3)
Neo-Nazis	2.56 (5)	2.94 (2)
Extreme Animal Rightists	2.54 (6)	2.79 (4)
Extreme Environmentalists	2.51 (7)	2.74 (5)
Ku Klux Klan	2.38 (8)	2.47 (8)
Left-Wing Revolutionaries	2.36 (9)	2.04 (14)
Extreme Anti-Abortion	2.36 (9)	2.30 (12)
Black Nationalists	2.34 (11)	2.35 (11)
Extreme Anti-Tax	2.33 (12)	2.47 (9)
Extreme Anti-Immigration	2.19 (13)	2.41 (10)
Christian Identity	2.19 (13)	2.59 (8)
Idiosyncratic Sectarians	2.19 (13)	2.13 (1)
Millennial/Doomsday Cults	2.17 (15)	1.93 (16)
Reconstructed Tratditions	2.13 (16)	2.04 (14)

(4) DHS again warns of domestic terrorism

This time DHS kept the report secret (so far), leaking their conclusions to friendly journalists at CNN:

> A new intelligence assessment, circulated by the Department of Homeland Security this month and reviewed by CNN, focuses on the domestic terror threat from right-wing sovereign citizen extremists and comes as the Obama administration holds a White House conference to focus efforts to fight violent extremism. Some federal and local law enforcement groups view the domestic terror threat from sovereign citizen groups as equal to — and in some cases greater than — the threat from foreign Islamic terror groups, such as ISIS, that garner more public attention.

> The Homeland Security report, produced in coordination with the FBI, counts 24 violent sovereign citizen-related attacks across the U.S. since 2010.

Twenty-four "violent attacks" over 4 years? The US had 16,121 people murdered in 2013.

(5) Rise of the Lone Wolf

A new report from the Southern Poverty Law Center: "Age of the Wolf." From the summary:

> The Southern Poverty Law Center is releasing a new study showing that domestic terrorism and related radical violence — as opposed to terrorist attacks emanating from abroad — continue to plague the nation. Our study also reveals that the vast majority of this violence is coming from "lone wolves" or "leaderless resistance" groups, most of the latter composed of just two men.

> The study, which covers the period between April 1, 2009, and Feb. 1, 2015, and includes violence from both the radical right and homegrown jihadists, finds that a domestic terrorist attack or foiled attack occurred, on average, every 34 days. It also shows that fully 74% of the more than 60 incidents examined were carried out, or planned, by a lone wolf, a single person

operating entirely alone. A total of 90% of the incidents were the work of just one or two persons, the study found.

The long-term trend away from violence planned and committed by groups and toward lone wolf terrorism is a worrying one. Authorities have had far more success penetrating plots concocted by several people than individuals who act on their own.

… A large number of independent studies have agreed that since the 9/11 mass murder, more people have been killed in America by non-Islamic domestic terrorists than jihadists. That fact is also apparent in the new SPLC study of the 2009-2015 period. Since 9/11, however, the government has focused very heavily on jihadists, sometimes to the exclusion of violence from various forms of domestic extremists.

What's the toll? Bad for the people and their families affected, but tiny for a nation of 319 million.

The body count of victims during the 2009-2015 period is certainly less than that of the 1990s, but that is heavily skewed by Timothy McVeigh's murder of 168 people in the 1995 Oklahoma City bombing. If the Oklahoma victims are subtracted, it appears that the rate of killing has remained approximately the same throughout. The SPLC study found that 63 victims had been killed in 2009-2015 terrorist attacks, along with 16 assailants. Another recent study, from the public-private National Consortium for the Study of Terrorism and Responses to Terrorism, or START, counted 368 people murdered by far-right extremists between 1990 and 2013, including 50 law enforcement officers. Without the Oklahoma victims, the START study (which did not include jihadists) shows an average killing rate of almost nine victims a year, while the SPLC study (including jihadists) finds an annual rate of almost 11.

(6) Conclusions

Since the early 1990s we have had occasional panic attacks about domestic terrorism, and (reasonably) more frequently since 9/11. The focus of our large and growing security services, to which they devote vast resources, is finding Islamic terrorists in the US—so rare that most found are manufactured by the FBI.

The US suffers from a more serious form of terrorism about which have less interest: from the Right (there is small-scale terrorism from the Left, which the police actively pursue). Conservatives actively work to block efforts to protect us from them. Should there be a major attack, we should assign responsibility accordingly.

The data clearly suggests a larger message: that domestic terrorism is among the least of the many threats to America—and one that our security services vigilantly cover—although detecting attacks in advance is an unrealistic goal (without a precrime unit). We have experienced many periods of low grade terrorism since the 19th century anarchists (in 1920 they almost blew the NYSE off the map). We'll experience more in the future. Let's not over-react.

Organizations to Contact

The editors have compiled the following list of organizations concerned with the issues debated in this book. The descriptions are derived from materials provided by the organizations. All have publications or information available for interested readers. The list was compiled on the date of publication of the present volume; the information provided here may change. Be aware that many organizations take several weeks or longer to respond to inquiries, so allow as much time as possible.

American Civil Liberties Union (ACLU)
125 Broad Street, 18th Floor
New York, NY 10004
(212) 549-2500
Website: http://www.aclu.org

Founded nearly 100 years ago, the ACLU is one of the largest American organizations dedicated to defending and preserving individual rights and liberties. The ACLU often fights for the rights of privacy of American citizens under the US Patriot Act.

The Department of Homeland Security
Washington, DC 20528
(202) 282-8000
Website: http://www.dhs.gov

The Department of Homeland Security is a cabinet of the US federal government set up to protect American civilians from threats within its borders. Jeh Johnson is the current US Secretary of Homeland Security.

The Federal Bureau of Investigation (FBI)

935 Pennsylvania Avenue NW
Washington, DC 20528
(800) 225-5324
online tips form: tips.fbi.gov
Website: http://www.fbi.gov

The FBI is a premier security and crime-fighting force that reports to both the attorney general and the director of national intelligence. It has dual responsibilities as both a law enforcement and intelligence agency and aims to protect the United States from terrorist attacks.

Homeland Security Watch

hlswatch@gmail.com
Website: http://www.hlswatch.com

This blog was founded by Christian Beckner is 2005 and is today a non-partisan organization that offers news, analysis, and commentary on critical issues in homeland security.

In Public Safety

LStelter@apus.edu
Website: http://inpublicsafety.com

In Public Safety is a blog-based organization sponsored by the American Military University (AMU). Its blog offers in-depth discussions on issues involving law enforcement and national intelligence, and training and educational opportunities for public safety professionals.

National Counterterrorism Center (NCTC)

1500 Tysons McLean Drive
McLean, VA 22102
nctcpao@nctc.gov
Website: https://www.nctc.gov

The National Counterterrorism Center (NCTC) was formed under Presidential Executive Order 13354 in 2004 as a way of bringing together personnel from various agencies in operational planning and intelligence. Today, the NCTC reports to the president of the United States and the director of national intelligence regarding intelligence and counterterrorism planning.

Office of the Director of National Intelligence (DNI)
Washington, DC 20511
(703) 733-8600
dni@ugov.gov
Website: http://www.dni.gov

The first national intelligence director was appointed by former president George W. Bush following the September 11, 2001, attacks in order to lead the integration of intelligence across various intelligence agencies. The fourth national intelligence director, the honorable James. R. Clapper, was sworn in to office in 2010.

The Office of Terrorism and Financial Intelligence (TFI)
Department of the Treasury
1500 Pennsylvania Avenue NW
Washington, DC 20220
(202) 622-2000
Website: http://www.treasury.gov/about/organizational
-structure/offices/Pages/Office-of-Terrorism-and-Financial
-Intelligence.aspx

Founded in 2014, this agency is under the purview of the US Department of the Treasury. It focuses on gathering information on financial crimes used by terrorist groups, particularly in regard to money launderers, drug cartels, and other security threats.

Office for Victims of Crime: Domestic Terrorism and Mass Violence

810 Seventh Street NW, Eighth Floor
Washington, DC 20531
Disaster Distress Helpline: (800) 985-5990
Text Hotline: 'TalkWithUs' to 66746
ITVERP@usdoj.gov
Website: http://www.ovc.gov/help/domestic_terrorism.html

The Office for Victims of Crime offers grief counseling, a 24/7 hotline, and information about investigations for those who have been affected by victims of domestic terrorism. The organization also works to get compensation for those affected by these crimes.

Southern Poverty Law Center (SPLC)

400 Washington Avenue
Montgomery, AL 36104
(888) 414-7752
Website: http://www.splcenter.org

The SPLC is a nonprofit organization that uses litigation, education, and other forms of advocacy to achieve its ideals of equal justice and equal opportunity for all. The SPLC has been instrumental in defending the rights of citizens in regard to US Patriot Act violations.

Bibliography

Books

JG Daniel. *Hate or Be Hated: How I Survived Right-Wing Extremism*. Oregon, WA: BookBaby, 2016.

Kevin Flynn and Barrie Swicker. *The Silent Brotherhood: The Chilling Inside Story of America's Violent, Anti-Government Militia Movement*. New York, NY: Signet, 2016.

Masha Gessen. *The Brothers: The Road to an American Tragedy*. New York, NY: Riverhead Books, 2016.

Christopher C. Harmon. *A Citizen's Guide to Terrorism and Counterterrorism*. New York, NY: Routledge, 2013.

Scott Helman and Jenna Russell. *Long Mile Home: Boston Under Attack, the City's Courageous Recovery, and the Epic Hunt for Justice*. New York, NY: NAL, 2014.

Douglas Kellner. *Guys and Guns Amok: Domestic Terrorism and School Shootings from the Oklahoma City Bombing to the Virginia Tech Massacre*. New York, NY: Routledge, 2008.

Daniel Levitas. *The Terrorist Next Door: The Militia Movement and the Radical Right*. New York, NY: Saint Martin's Griffin, 2004.

Donald R. Liddick. *Eco-Terrorism: Radical Environmental and Animal Liberation Movements*. Westport, CT: Praeger, 2006.

Lawrence E. Likar. *Eco-Warriors, Nihilistic Terrorists, and the Environment*. Westport, CT: Praeger, 2011.

Joseph T. McCann. *Terrorism on American Soil: A Concise History of Plots and Perpetrators from the Famous to the Forgotten*. Boulder, CO: Sentient Publications, 2006.

The Naval Postgraduate School. *Domestic Terrorism: Fighting the Local Threat with Local Enforcement*. CreateSpace, 2014.

Bob Navarro. *Acts of Domestic Terrorism in the United States.* CreateSpace, 2015.

Jeffrey D. Simon. *Lone Wolf Terrorism: Understanding the Growing Threat.* Amherst, NY: Prometheus Books, 2013.

Anne Speckhard and Mubin Shaikh. *Undercover Jihadi: Inside the Toronto 18—Al Qaeda Inspired, Homegrown Terrorism in the West.* Mclean, VA: Advances Press, 2014.

Jess Walter. *Every Knee Shall Bow: The Truth and Tragedy of Ruby Ridge and the Randy Weaver Family.* New York, NY: Harper, 1995.

Periodicals and Internet Sources

Richard E. Berkebile, "What Is Domestic Terrorism? A Method for Classifying Events from the Global Terrorism Database," *Terrorism and Political Violence*, February 2015. http://www .start.umd.edu/publication/what-domestic-terrorism -method-classifying-events-global-terrorism-database.

Jon Bowne, "DOJ Vies to Label Infowars as Domestic Terrorism," *InfoWars*, February 23, 2016. http://www .infowars.com/doj-vies-to-label-infowars-as-domestic -terrorism.

Juliegrace Brufke, "House Dems Race to Neutralize 'Right-Wing Domestic Terrorism,'" *World News Daily*, June 16, 2016. http://www.wnd.com/2016/06/house-dems-race-to -neutralize-right-wing-domestic-terrorism.

John Cassidy, "Domestic Terrorism and America's Gun Dilemma," *The New Yorker*, December 3, 2015. http://www .newyorker.com/news/john-cassidy/domestic-terrorism -and-americas-gun-dilemma.

Julia B. Chan and Scott Pham, "Lone Wolves Are the Face of Modern Domestic Terrorism," Reveal, June 18, 2016. https://www.revealnews.org/article/this-is-what-lone-wolf -terrorism-looks-like-in-the-us.

Noam Chomsky, "Domestic Terrorism: Notes on the State System of Oppression," *New Political Science*, September 1999. https://chomsky.info/199909.

Sivan Hirsch-Hoefler and Cas Mudde, "Ecoterrorism: Threat or Political Ploy?" *Washington* Post, December 14, 2014. https://www.washingtonpost.com/blogs/monkey-cage/wp/2014/12/19/ecoterrorism-threat-or-political-ploy.

Nick Jaynes, "Planned Parenthood Calls Colorado Shooting 'Domestic Terrorism,'" Mashable, November 27, 2015. http://mashable.com/2015/11/27/planned-parenthood-domestic-terrorism.

Charles Kurzman and Davis Schanzer, "The Growing Right-Wing Terror Threat," *New York Times*, June 16, 2015. http://www.nytimes.com/2015/06/16/opinion/the-other-terror-threat.html.

Bethania Palma Markus, "Reza Aslan: Anti-Muslim Hysteria Hides the True Threat of Homegrown Right-Wing Terrorism," *RawStory*, April 15, 2016. http://www.rawstory.com/2016/04/reza-aslan-anti-muslim-hysteria-hides-the-true-threat-of-homegrown-right-wing-terrorism.

Henry I. Miller and Jay Byme, "Domestic Eco-Terrorism Has Deep Pockets. And Many Enablers," *Forbes*, July 10, 2013. http://www.forbes.com/sites/henrymiller/2013/07/10/domestic-eco-terrorism-has-deep-pockets-and-many-enablers.

Robert A. Norton, "Food Defense in the Age of Domestic Terrorism," *FoodSafety*, December 15, 2015. http://www.foodsafetymagazine.com/enewsletter/food-defense-in-the-age-of-domestic-terrorism.

ThinkProgress, "Why Can't Anyone Agree on the Definition of 'Domestic Terrorism'?" ThinkProgress, December 9, 2015. https://thinkprogress.org/why-cant-anyone-agree-on-the-definition-of-domestic-terrorism-fed245151c42#.eqrza4362.

ThinkProgress, "You Are More Than 7 Times as Likely to
Be Killed by a Right-Wing Extremist Than by Muslim
Terrorists," ThinkProgress, November 30, 2015. https://
thinkprogress.org/you-are-more-than-7-times-as-likely
-to-be-killed-by-a-right-wing-extremist-than-by-muslim
-terrorists-417f3c3461db#.4nzt4qehy.

Index